THE ART OF
Great Cooking
WITH YOUR Instant Pot®

80 **INSPIRING, GLUTEN-FREE RECIPES** Made Easier, Faster
and More Nutritious in Your Multi-Function Cooker

EMILY SUNWELL-VIDAURRI
Founder of Recipes to Nourish

PAGE STREET
PUBLISHING CO.

PAGE STREET
PUBLISHING CO.

First published in 2017 by
Page Street Publishing Co.
27 Congress Street, Suite 105
Salem, MA 01970
www.pagestreetpublishing.com

Distributed by Macmillan, sales in Canada by The Canadian Manda Group.

21 20 19 18 17   1 2 3 4 5

ISBN-13: 978-1-62414-431-8
ISBN-10: 1-62414-431-4

Library of Congress Control Number: 2017937834

Cover and book design by Page Street Publishing Co.

Photography by Emily Sunwell-Vidaurri.
Author headshot on page 188 by Malissa Ann Photography.

Printed and bound in China

Instant Pot® is a registered trademark of Double Insight, Inc., which was not involved in the creation of this book.

As a member of 1% for the Planet, Page Street Publishing protects our planet by donating to nonprofits like The Trustees, which focuses on local land conservation. Learn more at onepercentfortheplanet.org.

TO MY HUSBAND, my best friend, my rock, my love.
Thank you for your support, your encouragement and your help
with this book. "So fortunate."

TO MY LITTLE LOVE AND TINY LOVE.
You fill my heart with sunshine every day.
I am so grateful to be your mommy.

IN LOVING MEMORY OF MY BEAUTIFUL MOM,
MARTHA CRISWELL, lover of truffle mousse pâté and St. André Brie,
the woman who taught me about gourmet food, broke out the Martha Stewart cookbooks
for her classy dinner parties and blasted Bonnie Raitt, The Judds, Carly Simon
and James Taylor as she decorated and cooked.

CONTENTS

Introduction

Everyone loves to enjoy a beautiful meal that's full of flavor and prepared with love. *The Art of Great Cooking with Your Instant Pot* showcases the preparation of nutritious ingredients to make stress-free meals. Whether you're cooking for your family or entertaining friends, these delicious recipes will make your loved ones feel cared for, honored and nourished.

My view of "great cooking" started with my mom. Her name was Martha, and she was "the" Martha Stewart in my eyes. I still remember the first gift I bought her with my own money: Martha Stewart's cookbooks on entertaining.

My mom loved to make things special, whether preparing food or decorating our home. She loved hosting small dinner parties and always made them fabulous. I adored watching her cook, putting so much love and care into the food. Then she'd make the house look perfect and dress up before the guests arrived. I wanted to be just like her.

I always thought the meals my mom prepared for those parties were magical. Crème caramel, truffle mousse pâté, parchment paper–wrapped chicken with julienned parsnips and carrots, mini currant muffin sandwiches with sliced turkey and preserves in the middle, layered ice cream sodas with fresh strawberry preserves and sparkling soda poured over the top. . . . I could go on and on about the gorgeous food memories I have that set the tone for what great cooking means to me.

So what is great cooking? It's probably different for everyone, but I think we can all agree that great cooking means making a meal special.

Great cooking doesn't have to mean overpriced foods or plates that are too dressed up. It can simply mean quality ingredients that are prepared and cooked to perfection, with thought given to where those ingredients came from and how they were raised or grown.

But great cooking doesn't have to be difficult. That's where the Instant Pot comes in.

The Instant Pot is a game-changer in the kitchen. Not only does it cook delicious food super-fast, but it locks in nutrition and makes food extremely tender and succulent. I want to show you that cooking with your Instant Pot can be easy, delicious and beautiful. You can use this amazing tool to speed up your prep time and get lovely meals on your table fast.

My husband is a fabulous cook who used to be a chef, and the Instant Pot has now become his favorite way to cook. He is accustomed to cooking things from scratch and he discovered that with the Instant Pot he could produce the same high-quality meals that he prepared before, but in half the time. We even have two Instant Pots . . . yes two! They're reasonably priced, and having a second one enables us to prepare main dishes at the same time as sides (or in some cases desserts), so the cooking goes even faster.

I love using the Instant Pot for everyday quick meals, and I also love it for special celebrations. I have saved so much time (and sanity!) using the Instant Pot to make gourmet meals for the holidays and other occasions.

The Instant Pot features a variety of settings that can accommodate just about any cooking style. Several different settings are used in this cookbook. You can even make a cake in it!

All the recipes in this cookbook are made with real, nourishing ingredients. You won't find any processed foods in here. My cooking style uses traditional foods—the real foods that our great-great-grandmothers cooked—and the Weston A. Price Foundation (WAPF)/Nourishing Traditions philosophy. In short, this means that I cook with whole foods. I also use the traditional practice of soaking beans and grains for better nutrition and digestion.

I believe in the importance of meats, dairy, eggs and healthy fats from grass-fed or pasture-raised animals, so that's what you will see in the recipes. "Grass-fed" and "pastured" imply that the animal was fed a species-appropriate diet, which in turn means it's healthier for you. This philosophy is all about honoring the way the food was produced and where it comes from. I prefer to buy from companies where I know the sourcing and practices. I also try to avoid the BPA present in most metal cans. For example, in several recipes I use crushed or whole tomatoes that are grown in Italy and sold in glass jars.

On a personal note, my body doesn't tolerate gluten. This means that the recipes in this cookbook are gluten-free, but you don't have to make them that way. Some recipes call for gluten-free ingredients such as tamari. Feel free to tailor these recipes to your own dietary needs.

All the soups and many other recipes call for bone broth because I try to pack as much nutrition as possible into any given dish. Bone broth is one of the most nourishing and healing foods you can consume. It's a nutrient-dense homemade broth that usually cooks for 24 hours, but have no fear, it does not take 24 hours in the Instant Pot! See my recipes on pages 116, 119 and 120 for easy Instant Pot bone broths. For my vegetarian friends, I've also included a nourishing vegetable stock (page 123) in the cookbook too.

I hope these recipes help take the stress out of cooking and help you bring back real, from-scratch home cooking for your family.

Emily Sunwell-Vidaurri

Hearty Beef, Pork & Lamb

Whether you're celebrating the day's events or craving shelter from life's storms, a warm, deeply-flavored meal at the end of the day can provide so much comfort. Hearty, meaty dishes are the kind of food my family turns to when we need stick-to-the-ribs nourishing food or just a meal that is sure to please. My family rarely dines out, so the dishes we prepare at home are made with care for a fine dining experience within the walls of our own home.

I love these meals because they instantly take me back to special times, celebrations or gatherings. The Traditional French Cassoulet (page 13) is one of those classic meals. It makes me think of dinner parties, where it's served family style to "oohs" and "ahhhs." I'm also crazy about the Bacon & Gruyère Crustless Quiche Lorraine (page 17) and the Sweet & Tangy "Baked" Ham (page 21). The quiche takes me back to the little French cafés that my mom and I frequented that served fancy quiches. The ham brings to mind holiday celebrations and family gatherings.

Sweet Grapes & Tarragon Pork Chops

Pork and fruit are meant for each other. Plain and simple. Slightly bittersweet tarragon and sweet juicy grapes add a fresh flavor to this quick and easy meal.

PREP TIME: 25 MINUTES | COOK TIME: 42 MINUTES | TOTAL TIME: 67 MINUTES | YIELD: 4 SERVINGS

5 tbsp (72 g) grass-fed butter, ghee or avocado oil, divided

2 lbs (907 g) bone-in pork chops

1 tsp sea salt, divided

2½ cups (230 g) red, green or black seedless grapes

1 red onion, sliced

4 fresh garlic cloves, minced

¼ cup (6 g) fresh tarragon leaves

1 tbsp (2 g) fresh thyme leaves

1 tbsp (21 g) honey

1 tbsp (15 ml) apple cider vinegar

1 cup (237 ml) chicken bone broth

1. Add 2 tablespoons (29 g) of healthy fat of choice to the Instant Pot and press "Sauté." Once the fat has melted, add the pork chops, sprinkle with ½ teaspoon of sea salt and brown for about 3½ minutes per side (you might have to do this in two batches depending on the size of the pork chops). Remove, transfer the browned pork chops to a plate and set aside. Add 1 tablespoon (14 g) of healthy fat of choice to the Instant Pot and add the grapes, sautéing until the grapes are lightly caramelized and starting to brown, about 5 minutes. Remove the grapes and set aside with the pork chops. Add the remaining 2 tablespoons (29 g) of healthy fat of choice, onion, garlic, tarragon, thyme and the remaining ½ teaspoon of sea salt, sautéing for 5 minutes, stirring occasionally. Press the "Keep Warm/Cancel" button. Add the honey, apple cider vinegar and bone broth and give it a good stir. Add the browned pork chops and ladle some of the liquid over the top. Place the lid on the Instant Pot, making sure the steam release valve is sealed. Press the "Meat/Stew" setting and decrease the time using the "-" button until you reach 25 minutes.

2. When the Instant Pot is done and beeps, press "Keep Warm/Cancel." Using an oven mitt, "quick release"/open the steam release valve. When the steam venting stops and the silver dial drops, carefully open the lid.

3. Plate the pork chops and allow to rest for 5 minutes. Serve immediately with the caramelized grapes, onions, tarragon and some of the cooking liquid.

NOTES

I use two small pork chops that fit in the Instant Pot. Keep the size of the Instant Pot in mind when purchasing the pork chops.

For a variation, leave the grapes on their stems. Pan-sauté them on the stove top in a skillet with 2 tablespoons (29 g) of grass-fed butter or ghee, flipping occasionally, until they start to caramelize and turn a light brown color, about 7 to 10 minutes. Add ½ cup (76 g) of sautéed grapes to the recipe, reserving the rest on their stems for plating with the pork chops.

Traditional French Cassoulet

This traditional casserole originated in the south of France. It's a rich, hearty dish full of beautiful meats and creamy white beans. The beans are soaked prior to cooking for better nutrition and easier digestion.

INACTIVE PREP TIME: 24 HOURS | PREP TIME: 30 MINUTES | COOK TIME: 35 MINUTES | TOTAL TIME: 65 MINUTES | YIELD: 6–8 SERVINGS

SOAKED WHITE BEANS

1 cup (201 g) dried white beans

1 tbsp (15 ml) apple cider vinegar or lemon juice

Pinch baking soda

Filtered water

FRENCH CASSOULET

3 tbsp (43 g) grass-fed butter, ghee or avocado oil, divided

2 chicken leg quarters

2 chicken thighs or legs

4 pork sausages

1½ tsp (4 g) sea salt, divided

1 yellow onion, diced

8 fresh garlic cloves, minced

5 fresh thyme sprigs, leaves removed and stems discarded

1 fresh bay leaf

4 oz (113 g) pre-cooked crispy pastured bacon, chopped

¼ cup (10 g) fresh Italian parsley, chopped

2 carrots, peeled and cut into large 2" (5-cm) pieces

7 sun-dried tomatoes

4 whole peeled tomatoes

4 cups (946 ml) chicken bone broth

¼ cup (6 g) fresh Italian parsley, roughly chopped, for garnish

Extra-virgin olive oil, for garnish

1. To soak the beans, add the dry beans to a large stock pot along with 1 tablespoon (15 ml) of apple cider vinegar or lemon juice and a pinch of baking soda. Fill the stockpot with three times more water than beans (3 cups [709 ml]). Bring to a light simmer on the stove, then remove from the heat, cover the pot and let the beans soak for a minimum of 8 hours, but preferably overnight for 12 to 24 hours. With a spoon, remove any bubbles or scum that floats to the top. Drain and rinse the beans in a colander, making sure they get rinsed very well.

2. Add 2 tablespoons (29 g) of healthy fat of choice to the Instant Pot and press "Sauté." Once the fat has melted, add the chicken and sausages, sprinkle with ½ teaspoon of sea salt and brown for about 2½ minutes per side (you might have to do this in two batches). Remove the browned chicken and sausages, transfer to a plate and set aside. Add the onion, garlic, thyme, bay leaf and remaining sea salt, sautéing for 7 minutes, stirring occasionally until lightly caramelized. Press the "Keep Warm/Cancel" button. Add the drained and rinsed soaked beans, browned chicken and sausages, cooked crispy bacon, parsley, carrots, sun-dried tomatoes, whole tomatoes and bone broth in that order. Place the lid on the Instant Pot, making sure the steam release valve is sealed. Press the "Poultry" setting, then increase the time using the "+" button until you reach 23 minutes.

3. When the Instant Pot is done and beeps, press "Keep Warm/Cancel." Allow the Instant Pot pressure to release naturally for 5 minutes. Using an oven mitt, "quick release"/open the steam release valve. When the steam venting stops and the silver dial drops, carefully open the lid.

4. Serve immediately, garnished with chopped Italian parsley and a generous drizzle of extra-virgin olive oil.

NOTES

The traditional practice of soaking beans helps reduce or neutralize phytic acid. This process helps with digestion and makes the beans more nutrient-dense. If you're pressed for time, canned beans can be substituted for soaked beans.

I use whole peeled tomatoes, grown in Italy, that come in tomato purée in a glass jar.

Provençal Green Olive Tapenade Leg of Lamb

The homemade tapenade, paired with this tender lamb, is incredible. The lamb is already amazing with lots of fresh herbs and garlic, but with the salty, flavorful tapenade it is out of this world.

PREP TIME: 35 MINUTES | COOK TIME: 46 MINUTES | TOTAL TIME: 81 MINUTES | YIELD: 4 SERVINGS

LEG OF LAMB

3 tbsp (43 g) grass-fed butter, ghee or avocado oil, divided

1 lb (454 g) leg of lamb bone-in steaks

1¼ tsp (4 g) sea salt, divided

1 yellow onion, sliced

6 fresh garlic cloves, minced

3 tbsp (7 g) fresh rosemary leaves, finely chopped

3 tbsp (10 g) fresh thyme leaves

½ tsp freshly cracked black pepper

1 cup (237 ml) chicken bone broth

GREEN OLIVE TAPENADE

1 cup (180 g) pitted green olives

¼ cup (15 g) sun-dried tomatoes

¼ cup (59 ml) extra-virgin olive oil or avocado oil

3 tbsp (26 g) capers

2 tbsp (30 ml) fresh lemon juice

2 tbsp (4 g) fresh thyme leaves

1 tbsp (3 g) fresh Italian parsley

1 fresh garlic clove

½ tsp anchovy paste

1. Add 1 tablespoon (14 g) of healthy fat of choice to the Instant Pot and press "Sauté." Once the fat has melted, add the lamb, sprinkle with ¼ teaspoon of sea salt and brown for about 3 minutes per side. Remove the browned lamb to a plate and set aside. Add the remaining 2 tablespoons (29 g) of healthy fat of choice, onion, garlic, rosemary, thyme, black pepper and the remaining 1 teaspoon of sea salt, sautéing for 5 minutes, stirring occasionally. Press the "Keep Warm/Cancel" button. Add the bone broth and give it a good stir. Add the browned lamb, making sure it's submerged and some of the liquid has been ladled over it. Place the lid on the Instant Pot, making sure the steam release valve is sealed. Press the "Meat" setting for 35 minutes.

2. While the lamb is cooking, make the tapenade. Place all ingredients in a food processor or blender. Pulse until everything is roughly chopped, but not fully puréed. Set aside.

3. When the Instant Pot is done and beeps, press "Keep Warm/Cancel." Using an oven mitt, "quick release"/open the steam release valve. When the steam venting stops and the silver dial drops, carefully open the lid.

4. Plate the lamb and allow it to rest for 5 minutes. Serve immediately with a generous amount of green olive tapenade.

NOTES

I use two small bone-in lamb leg steaks that fit in the Instant Pot. Keep the size of the Instant Pot in mind when purchasing the lamb. If you're using a larger cut of meat, make sure to increase the cooking time to about 45 minutes.

If you end up having any leftover tapenade, it's wonderful with other meat or white fish dishes as well as slathered on crusty bread, crackers or fresh veggies.

Bacon & Gruyère Crustless Quiche Lorraine

Quiche Lorraine was my mom's all-time favorite quiche, so it holds a special place in my heart. Named after a region in France, Quiche Lorraine is a classic. With a creamy custard filling, this tantalizing quiche is stuffed with crispy bacon, salty ham and two buttery cheeses.

PREP TIME: 25 MINUTES | COOK TIME: 27 MINUTES | TOTAL TIME: 52 MINUTES | YIELD: 6 SERVINGS

2 tbsp (29 g) grass-fed butter or ghee, plus more for greasing dish

1 small yellow onion, diced

2 fresh garlic cloves, grated or finely minced

½ tsp dried thyme

6 pastured eggs

½ cup (118 ml) cream

1 tsp sea salt

½ cup (75 g) sliced ham, diced

6 slices precooked crispy pastured bacon, crumbled

½ cup (60 g) shredded gruyère

½ cup (60 g) shredded aged or sharp cheddar cheese

1 cup (237 ml) water

1. Add butter to the Instant Pot and press "Sauté." Once the fat has melted, add the onion, garlic and thyme, sautéing for 7 minutes until lightly caramelized. Press the "Keep Warm/Cancel" button.

2. With butter, grease a 1½-quart (1.5-L) casserole dish (I use one with a glass lid) that fits inside the Instant Pot. Set it aside. In a large mixing bowl, whisk the eggs and cream together until the eggs are fully incorporated. Add the sea salt, ham, bacon, ¾ of the cheese and the onion-herb mixture, gently stirring to combine. Pour the mixture into the greased casserole dish. Place the glass lid on top of the casserole dish. Place the Instant Pot trivet inside the Instant Pot. Pour 1 cup (237 ml) of water into the Instant Pot. Carefully transfer the covered casserole dish into the Instant Pot on top of the trivet. Place the lid on the Instant Pot, making sure the steam release valve is sealed. Press the "Manual" setting and decrease the time using the "-" button until you reach 20 minutes.

3. When the Instant Pot is done and beeps, press "Keep Warm/Cancel." Allow the Instant Pot to release pressure naturally for 10 minutes. Using an oven mitt, "quick release"/open the steam release valve. When the steam venting stops and the silver dial drops, carefully open the lid.

4. Carefully remove the casserole dish from the Instant Pot and remove the lid from the dish. Next, add the leftover cheese to the top of the quiche and either place the dish back in the Instant Pot for about 3 minutes to melt the cheese, or place it under a preheated broiler in the oven for about 3 to 5 minutes to brown the cheese.

5. Serve hot or warm.

NOTE

For this quiche, you will need a 1½-quart (1.5-L) casserole dish or a 6-cup (1.5-L) heat-safe glass or stainless steel bowl that fits inside the Instant Pot. You will also need a lid. I use a casserole dish that comes with a glass lid. If you don't have a lid for your dish or bowl, you can place a piece of parchment paper over the top of the quiche, then cover it securely with foil.

Greek Stuffed Bell Peppers

These Greek-inspired bell peppers burst with refreshing flavors. They're packed with herby aromatics, delicate jasmine rice, sweet juicy raisins, zesty lemon, and creamy Mizithra and feta cheeses, with perfectly steamed bell pepper in every bite.

PREP TIME: 25 MINUTES | COOK TIME: 22 MINUTES | TOTAL TIME: 47 MINUTES | YIELD: 4 SERVINGS

2 tbsp (29 g) grass-fed butter, ghee or avocado oil, plus butter for greasing dish

1 small yellow onion, diced

4 fresh garlic cloves, grated or finely minced

1 lb (454 g) grass-fed ground beef or lamb

1 cup (186 g) cooked jasmine rice

1 pastured egg

2 tsp (11 g) tomato paste

1¼ tsp (4 g) sea salt

Zest of 1 lemon

½ cup (12 g) chopped fresh mint

⅓ cup (10 g) chopped fresh Italian parsley, plus more for garnish

⅓ cup (48 g) raisins

¾ cup (75 g) grated mizithra or parmigiano-reggiano, plus more for garnish

½ cup (75 g) crumbled feta cheese

4 red bell peppers, tops removed and seeded

1 cup (237 ml) water

1. Add healthy fat of choice to the Instant Pot and press "Sauté." Once the fat has melted, add the onion and garlic, sautéing for 7 minutes until lightly caramelized. Press the "Keep Warm/Cancel" button.

2. With butter, grease a 1½-quart (1.5-L) casserole dish (I use one with a glass lid) that fits inside the Instant Pot. Set aside.

3. To a large mixing bowl, add the ground beef, cooked rice, egg, tomato paste, sea salt, lemon zest, mint, parsley, raisins, cheeses and onion-garlic mixture. Gently mix until everything is combined. Evenly divide and stuff the meat filling into the bell peppers. Transfer the stuffed bell peppers to the casserole dish. Place the glass lid on top of the casserole dish. Place the Instant Pot trivet inside the Instant Pot. Pour 1 cup (237 ml) of water into the Instant Pot. Carefully transfer the covered casserole dish to the Instant Pot on top of the trivet. Place the lid on the Instant Pot, making sure the steam release valve is sealed. Press the "Manual" setting and decrease the time using the "-" button until you reach 15 minutes.

4. When the Instant Pot is done and beeps, press "Keep Warm/Cancel." Allow the Instant Pot to release pressure naturally for 15 minutes. Using an oven mitt, "quick release"/open the steam release valve. When the steam venting stops and the silver dial drops, carefully open the lid.

5. Carefully remove the casserole dish from the Instant Pot and remove the lid.

6. Serve the stuffed peppers topped with freshly grated mizithra or parmigiano-reggiano and freshly chopped parsley.

NOTES

You will need a 1½-quart (1.5-L) casserole dish that fits in the Instant Pot. You will also need a lid. I use a casserole dish that comes with a glass lid. If you don't have a lid for your dish or bowl, you can place a piece of parchment paper over the top, then cover it securely with foil.

Try using green or yellow bell peppers instead of red bell peppers.

Sweet & Tangy "Baked" Ham

My Tiny Love and husband really love ham, so I'm always looking for ways to make it special for them. I admit, ham isn't always my favorite, but sweet and tangy "baked" ham, well, now we're talking! This shredded ham is crazy good and it's always a crowd (or little hands) pleaser.

PREP TIME: 25 MINUTES | COOK TIME: 63 MINUTES | TOTAL TIME: 88 MINUTES | YIELD: 10–12 SERVINGS

3 lb (1.4 kg) half-cut cooked boneless ham, cut into large 2" (5-cm) chunks (not spiral)

3 cups (710 ml) filtered water

1 cup (237 ml) apple cider vinegar

½ cup (118 ml) maple syrup

3 tbsp (64 g) honey

3 tsp (16 g) Dijon or horseradish mustard

1 tsp fresh thyme, chopped

Pinch ground cinnamon

1. Place the ham chunks in the Instant Pot. Cover with the water and apple cider vinegar. If your ham isn't fully covered, add more water and apple cider vinegar, being careful not to exceed the max fill line. Place the lid on the Instant Pot, making sure the steam release valve is sealed. Press the "Meat/Stew" setting and increase the time using the "+" button until you reach 33 minutes.

2. When the Instant Pot is done and beeps, press "Keep Warm/Cancel." Allow the Instant Pot to release pressure naturally for 15 minutes. Using an oven mitt, "quick release"/open the steam release valve. When the steam venting stops and the silver dial drops, carefully open the lid.

3. Carefully remove the ham chunks and pull apart into shredded pieces. Pour the cooking liquid out of the Instant Pot and discard. Add the shredded ham back to the Instant Pot. Add the maple syrup, honey, mustard, thyme and cinnamon and stir to combine, making sure all the ham gets coated. Place the lid back on the Instant Pot, making sure the steam release valve is sealed. Press the "Keep Warm/Cancel" button and increase the time with the "+" button until you reach 30 minutes. After it has warmed for 30 minutes, press the "Keep Warm/Cancel" button again to turn off the Instant Pot. Use an oven mitt to open the steam release valve just for safety. The silver dial should already be dropped, but it's still important to carefully open the lid.

4. Pour the ham into a shallow dish and allow the juices to set up and absorb into the ham.

5. Serve the ham hot or cold.

Gruyère & Ham Potatoes au Gratin

There's nothing like a beautiful meal of layered potatoes with lots of nutty gruyère and aged cheddar, studded with green onions and bits of salty ham with a garlicky cream sauce. The Instant Pot makes cooking Potatoes au Gratin so easy.

PREP TIME: 25 MINUTES | COOK TIME: 50 MINUTES | TOTAL TIME: 75 MINUTES | YIELD: 6 SERVINGS

2 tbsp (29 g) grass-fed butter or ghee, plus some butter for greasing dish

1 shallot, diced

4 fresh garlic cloves, grated or finely minced

1 tsp sea salt

2 cups (473 ml) cream

3 russet potatoes, peeled and sliced ⅛" (3 mm) thick

2 green onions, diced

6 oz (170 g) sliced ham, diced

1 cup (120 g) shredded gruyère

½ cup (60 g) shredded aged or sharp cheddar cheese

¼ cup (45 g) shredded parmigiano-reggiano cheese

1 cup (237 ml) water

1. In a saucepan over medium heat, add the butter, shallot, garlic and sea salt, sautéing for 5 minutes. Add the cream and bring to a simmer for 2 minutes, then remove from heat.

2. With butter, grease a 1½-quart (1.5-L) casserole dish (I use one with a glass lid) that fits inside the Instant Pot. Layer the potatoes, green onions, ham and cheeses (reserving ¼ cup [28 g] cheese mixture for the top) repeating until finished, making sure to leave at least 1" (2.5 cm) space at the top of the casserole dish. Pour the onion-cream sauce over the top of the layered potatoes. Place the glass lid on top of the casserole dish. Place the Instant Pot trivet inside the Instant Pot. Pour 1 cup (237 ml) of water into the Instant Pot. Carefully add the covered casserole dish to the Instant Pot on top of the trivet. Place the lid on the Instant Pot, making sure the steam release valve is sealed. Press the "Manual" setting and increase the time with the "+" button until you reach 40 minutes.

3. When the Instant Pot is done and beeps, press "Keep Warm/Cancel." Allow the Instant Pot to release pressure naturally for 15 minutes. Using an oven mitt, "quick release"/open the steam release valve. When the steam venting stops and the silver dial drops, carefully open the lid.

4. Carefully remove the casserole dish from the Instant Pot and remove the lid. Next, add the reserved cheese to the top of the gratin and either place the casserole dish back in the Instant Pot for about 3 minutes to melt the cheese or place under a preheated broiler for 3 to 5 minutes until the cheese is bubbly and golden brown.

5. Serve hot.

NOTES

For a vibrant topping, garnish with fresh chopped chives.

You will need a 1½-quart (1.5-L) casserole dish or a 6-cup (1.5-L) heat-safe glass or stainless steel bowl that fits in the Instant Pot for this gratin. You will also need a lid. I use a casserole dish that comes with a glass lid. If you don't have a lid for your dish or bowl, you can place a piece of parchment paper over the top, then cover it securely with foil.

Braised Lemongrass Meatballs

Meatballs are always a favorite in my home. With garlic, zingy ginger, vibrant cilantro and sweet mint, these little bites are bursting with flavor. They're braised in a coconut water bath that's kissed with citrusy lemongrass, and they cook in minutes.

PREP TIME: 25 MINUTES | COOK TIME: 15 MINUTES | TOTAL TIME: 40 MINUTES | YIELD: 4–6 SERVINGS

1 lb (454 g) grass-fed ground beef

1½ tsp (4 g) garlic powder

¾ tsp sea salt

½ tsp ground ginger

3 tbsp (4 g) chopped fresh cilantro, plus more for garnish

3 tbsp (4 g) chopped fresh mint, plus more for garnish

1 pastured egg

¾ cup (177 ml) coconut water

¼ cup (59 ml) coconut aminos or gluten-free tamari

1 full-length stem of lemongrass, cut in half lengthwise and quartered

1 fresh garlic clove, smashed

1. In a large mixing bowl, combine the ground beef, garlic powder, sea salt, ginger, cilantro, mint and egg. Very gently mix until everything is incorporated and evenly distributed. Roll the mixture into small meatballs about 1" (3 cm) in diameter. Set them aside on a plate.

2. Add the coconut water, aminos, lemongrass and smashed garlic to the Instant Pot. Gently place the meatballs into the braising liquid, making sure to ladle some of the liquid over the meatballs. Place the lid on the Instant Pot, making sure the steam release valve is sealed. Press the "Manual" setting, then decrease the time with the "-" button until you reach 15 minutes.

3. When the Instant Pot is done and beeps, press "Keep Warm/Cancel." Allow it to release pressure naturally for 15 minutes. Using an oven mitt, "quick release"/open the steam release valve. When the steam venting stops and the silver dial drops, carefully open the lid.

4. Serve immediately, topped with freshly chopped cilantro and mint.

> **NOTE**
> These are delicious served with steamed jasmine rice—buttered, coconut flavored or studded with cilantro or mint. They're also great made into lettuce wraps.

Honey-Braised Lamb Shanks

These succulent lamb shanks are perfect for an intimate dinner party or romantic dinner for two. The tender meat is cooked in a honey sauce infused with fennel and citrus.

PREP TIME: 15 MINUTES | COOK TIME: 45 MINUTES | TOTAL TIME: 60 MINUTES | YIELD: 4 SERVINGS

4 tbsp (57 g) grass-fed butter, ghee or avocado oil, divided

2 lamb shanks (small enough to fit in your Instant Pot)

1½ tsp (4 g) sea salt, divided

1 yellow onion, diced

3 fresh garlic cloves, minced

2 tsp (4 g) fennel seed

2 sprigs rosemary

¼ cup (85 g) honey

5 oz (142 g) pitted green olives

¾ cup (177 ml) fresh orange juice

¼ cup (59 ml) fresh lemon juice

1. Add 2 tablespoons (29 g) of healthy fat of choice to the Instant Pot and press "Sauté." Once the fat has melted, add the lamb shanks, sprinkle with ½ teaspoon of sea salt and brown on each side, about 2½ minutes per side. Remove the browned lamb shanks to a plate and set aside. Add the remaining 2 tablespoons (29 g) of healthy fat of choice to the Instant Pot and add the onion, garlic, fennel seed and rosemary sprigs, sautéing for 5 minutes, stirring occasionally. Press the "Keep Warm/Cancel" button. Add the honey and give it a quick stir until it's mostly melted. Add the green olives, orange juice, lemon juice and remaining 1 teaspoon sea salt. Stir to combine, then add the browned lamb shanks. Place the lid on the Instant Pot, making sure the steam release valve is sealed. Press the "Meat" setting for 35 minutes.

2. When the Instant Pot is done and beeps, press "Keep Warm/Cancel." Allow the Instant Pot to release pressure naturally for 10 minutes. Using an oven mitt, "quick release"/open the steam release valve. When the steam venting stops and the silver dial drops, carefully open the lid.

3. Serve immediately with some of the sweet honey sauce ladled on top.

> **NOTE**
> My family loves to eat this with a simple creamy polenta. It's also delicious served with baked potatoes or small pasta.

Caramelized Apple & Fennel-Garlic-Herb Pork Loin

A beautiful meal to serve to guests, this appetizing pork loin is well-seasoned with fresh rosemary, thyme and garlic. Paired with lots of caramelized apples and fennel, it is sure to be a hit. It's easy enough to prepare for a weeknight meal, too.

PREP TIME: 25 MINUTES | COOK TIME: 47 MINUTES | TOTAL TIME: 72 MINUTES | YIELD: 4 SERVINGS

5 tbsp (72 g) grass-fed butter, ghee or avocado oil, divided

3 apples, halved, cored and sliced

1 fennel bulb, white bulb only, cored and thinly sliced

1½ lbs (680 g) pork loin

1¼ tsp (4 g) sea salt, divided

1 yellow onion, sliced

5 fresh garlic cloves, minced

2 tbsp (4 g) finely chopped fresh rosemary leaves

1 tbsp (2 g) fresh thyme leaves

1 cup (237 ml) chicken bone broth

1. Add 2 tablespoons (29 g) of healthy fat of choice to the Instant Pot and press "Sauté." Once the fat has melted, add the apple and fennel slices, sautéing for about 8 minutes until they're lightly caramelized and golden brown. Carefully remove the caramelized apples and fennel to a plate and set aside.

2. Add 1 tablespoon (14 g) of healthy fat of choice and the pork loin, sprinkle with ¼ teaspoon of sea salt and brown for about 3½ minutes per side. Remove the browned pork loin to a plate and set aside. Add the remaining 2 tablespoons (29 g) of healthy fat of choice, onion, garlic, rosemary, thyme and the remaining 1 teaspoon of sea salt, sautéing for 7 minutes, stirring occasionally. Press the "Keep Warm/Cancel" button. Add the bone broth and give everything a good stir. Add the browned pork loin, making sure it's submerged. Ladle some of the liquid over the top. Place the lid on the Instant Pot, making sure the steam release valve is sealed. Press the "Meat/Stew" setting and decrease the time using the "-" button until you reach 25 minutes.

3. When the Instant Pot is done and beeps, press "Keep Warm/Cancel." Using an oven mitt, "quick release"/open the steam release valve. When the steam venting stops and the silver dial drops, carefully open the lid.

4. Plate the pork loin and allow it to rest for 5 minutes. Carefully pour the remaining liquid into a jar. While the pork loin is resting, reheat the caramelized apples and fennel in the Instant Pot using the "Sauté" feature or on the stove top. Once the pork loin has rested, slice the meat on a bias about ¾" (2 cm) thick. Serve immediately with the caramelized apples and fennel along with some of the cooking liquid.

> **NOTES**
> Keep the size of the Instant Pot in mind when purchasing the pork loin.
>
> If you'd like to save time, you can also sauté and caramelize the apples and fennel on the stove while your pork loin is cooking in the Instant Pot.

Asian Pear Korean-Braised Short Ribs

Braised short ribs are elegant, and they're not hard to make in the Instant Pot. These flavorful, perfectly sweet, tender, fall-apart grass-fed short ribs are sure to please.

PREP TIME: 25 MINUTES | COOK TIME: 46 MINUTES | TOTAL TIME: 71 MINUTES | YIELD: 4–6 SERVINGS

3 tbsp (43 g) grass-fed butter, ghee or avocado oil

2 lbs (907 g) grass-fed bone-in short ribs

¾ tsp sea salt

13 pearl onions, peeled, or 1 red onion, peeled and thickly sliced

6 fresh garlic cloves, minced

2 Asian pears, peeled, cored and quartered

⅓ cup (79 ml) maple syrup or honey

⅓ cup (79 ml) coconut aminos or gluten-free tamari

¼ cup (59 ml) apple cider vinegar

½ cup (118 ml) beef or chicken bone broth

3 carrots, peeled and cut into large 2" (5-cm) pieces

1 large daikon radish, cut into large 2" (5-cm) pieces

1. Add healthy fat of choice to the Instant Pot and press "Sauté." Once the fat has melted, add the short ribs, season with the sea salt and brown on each side, about 3 minutes per side. Remove the browned short ribs to a plate and set aside. Add the onions and garlic, sautéing for 5 minutes, stirring occasionally. Press the "Keep Warm/Cancel" button.

2. To a blender add the Asian pear pieces, maple syrup or honey, aminos or tamari, apple cider vinegar and bone broth. Blend on low speed just until the Asian pear is liquefied.

3. Transfer the short ribs, carrots and radish to the Instant Pot and cover with the Asian pear sauce. Place the lid on the Instant Pot, making sure the steam release valve is sealed. Press the "Meat/Stew" setting for 35 minutes.

4. When the Instant Pot is done and beeps, press "Keep Warm/Cancel." Using an oven mitt, "quick release"/open the steam release valve. When the steam venting stops and the silver dial drops, carefully open the lid.

5. Remove the short ribs and plate on a serving dish with the carrots, radish, onions and Asian pear sauce.

NOTES

The leftover Asian pear sauce is delicious when reduced. Leave the liquid in the Instant Pot and use the "Sauté" feature to bring the liquid to a boil. Let it boil, stirring occasionally, until it reduces by half, 7 to 10 minutes.

Bacon-Wrapped Molasses Pork Tenderloin

Tender, juicy meat doused in dark, sticky, robust molasses, sweet maple syrup and spicy ginger with hints of apricot all wrapped with salty, smoky bacon. This bacon-wrapped pork tenderloin is stellar!

INACTIVE PREP TIME: 4 HOURS | PREP TIME: 25 MINUTES | COOK TIME: 34 MINUTES | TOTAL TIME: 59 MINUTES | YIELD: 4 SERVINGS

3 tbsp (44 ml) maple syrup

2 tbsp (42 g) organic blackstrap molasses

½ cup (118 ml) coconut aminos or gluten-free tamari

3 tbsp (60 g) apricot jam

2" (5-cm) knob fresh ginger, peeled and finely minced or grated

1 sprig rosemary, leaves removed and chopped

1 lb (454 g) pork tenderloin

6 pastured bacon slices

2 tbsp (29 g) grass-fed butter, ghee or avocado oil

½ tsp sea salt

½ cup (118 ml) chicken bone broth

1. In a mixing bowl, combine the maple syrup, molasses, aminos, apricot jam, ginger and rosemary. Pour into a large bowl or marinating bag, add the pork tenderloin and marinate for at least 1 hour, up to 4 hours.

2. Remove the pork tenderloin from the marinade and wrap it with bacon, using toothpicks to secure the bacon. Add healthy fat of choice to the Instant Pot and press "Sauté." Once the fat has melted, add the bacon-wrapped pork tenderloin and brown on each side, about 3½ minutes per side. Press the "Keep Warm/Cancel" button. Add ½ cup (118 ml) of the marinade, the salt and the bone broth, ladling some of the marinade over the top. Place the lid on the Instant Pot, making sure the steam release valve is sealed. Press "Meat/Stew" setting and decrease the time using the "-" button until you reach 22 minutes.

3. When the Instant Pot is done and beeps, press "Keep Warm/Cancel." Using an oven mitt, "quick release"/open the steam release valve. When the steam venting stops and the silver dial drops, carefully open the lid.

4. Optional: For crispier bacon, transfer the tenderloin to a baking sheet and place it on the middle rack under a broiler for 3 to 5 minutes.

5. Plate the pork tenderloin and allow it to rest for 5 minutes before serving.

> **NOTE**
> Keep the size of the Instant Pot in mind when purchasing the pork tenderloin.

Sauerkraut-Apple Pork Roast

Pork with sauerkraut is said to bring good luck when served on New Year's, but that doesn't mean it should be served only once a year. Overflowing with fermented kraut and delicate caramelized apples, this tender, shredded roast has the perfect combination of tangy and sweet.

PREP TIME: 25 MINUTES | COOK TIME: 57 MINUTES | TOTAL TIME: 82 MINUTES | YIELD: 6–8 SERVINGS

4 tbsp (57 g) grass-fed butter, ghee or avocado oil, divided

3 apples, cored and sliced

2–3 lbs (907–1361 g) pork roast

1 yellow onion, sliced

4 fresh garlic cloves, minced

1 tbsp (21 g) honey

½ sprig rosemary, leaves removed and chopped

1½ tsp (4 g) sea salt

1 cup (237 ml) apple cider

4 cups (578 g) fermented sauerkraut, divided

NOTES

Keep the size of the Instant Pot in mind when purchasing the pork roast.

If you don't have apple cider on hand, you can substitute chicken bone broth.

Fermented sauerkraut is easy to find at natural food stores and mainstream grocery stores. Just look for authentic fermented sauerkraut. It should say "fermented" or "live cultures" or "probiotic-rich" on the label.

1. Add 2 tablespoons (29 g) of healthy fat of choice to the Instant Pot and press "Sauté." Once the fat has melted, add the apple slices, sautéing for about 8 minutes, stirring occasionally until they're lightly caramelized and golden brown. Carefully remove the caramelized apples to a plate and set aside. This can also be done on the stove in a saucepan if you'd prefer.

2. Add 2 tablespoons (29 g) of healthy fat of choice to the Instant Pot and press "Sauté." Once the fat has melted, add the pork roast and brown for about 3½ minutes per side. Remove the roast and transfer to a plate. Set aside. Add the onion, garlic, honey, rosemary and sea salt, sautéing for 2 minutes until fragrant. Press the "Keep Warm/Cancel" button. Add the apple cider, give it a stir, then carefully add the browned pork roast. Place the lid on the Instant Pot, making sure the steam release valve is sealed. Press "Meat/Stew" for 35 minutes.

3. When the Instant Pot is done and beeps, press "Keep Warm/Cancel." Allow the Instant Pot to release pressure naturally for 15 minutes. Using an oven mitt, "quick release"/open the steam release valve. When the steam venting stops and the silver dial drops, carefully open the lid.

4. Add 2 cups (284 g) of the sauerkraut, reserving the remaining 2 cups (284 g) for serving, and place the lid on the Instant Pot, making sure the steam release valve is sealed. Press "Manual" and decrease the time using the "-" button until you reach 5 minutes.

5. When the Instant Pot is done and beeps, press "Keep Warm/Cancel." Using an oven mitt, "quick release"/open the steam release valve. When the steam venting stops and the silver dial drops, carefully open the lid. Add the caramelized apples to the top of the roast. Place the lid on the Instant Pot and allow it to rest for 5 minutes to warm the apples.

6. Shred the pork roast and serve immediately with caramelized apples, cooked kraut and reserved raw sauerkraut (so you get the naturally occurring probiotics).

German Beef Rouladen

This traditional German beef roll is made with thinly pounded beef slathered with spicy mustard and fragrant herby, garlicky onions and then rolled up with fermented pickles and cooked in a delicious gravy sauce. It's a fabulous dish to serve on special occasions.

PREP TIME: 30 MINUTES | COOK TIME: 61 MINUTES | TOTAL TIME: 91 MINUTES | YIELD: 4–6 SERVINGS

4 tbsp (57 g) grass-fed butter, ghee or avocado oil, divided

1 yellow onion, diced

4 fresh garlic cloves, minced

1½ tsp (4 g) sea salt, divided

2 tbsp (6 g) minced fresh dill

1 tsp minced fresh thyme leaves

1 tsp minced fresh rosemary leaves

1½ lbs (680 g) flank steak, pounded ⅛–¼" (3–6 mm) thick and cut into filets about 4" (10 cm) wide

2 tbsp (31 g) Dijon or horseradish mustard

2 fermented pickles, cut in half and then into spears

1 cup (237 ml) beef bone broth or pickle juice

2 tbsp (26 g) flour of choice or 1 tbsp (8 g) cornstarch mixed with 1 tbsp (15 ml) filtered water

Fresh Italian parsley, chopped, for garnish

NOTE
This meal is delicious served with fermented sauerkraut, steamed or roasted beets and baked or mashed potatoes.

1. Add 2 tablespoons (29 g) of healthy fat of choice to the Instant Pot and press "Sauté." Once the fat has melted, add the onion, garlic and ½ teaspoon of sea salt, sautéing for 7 minutes, stirring occasionally until lightly caramelized. Add the dill, thyme and rosemary and continue to sauté for 2 minutes, giving it a good stir. Press the "Keep Warm/Cancel" button and let the mixture sit while you prep the beef rolls.

2. Prep each piece of pounded beef on a flat surface. Season with ½ teaspoon sea salt. Evenly divide the mustard among the 4 pieces of meat and spread over one side of each piece. Evenly divide and spoon the onion-garlic-herb mixture over the meat, spreading it out in a flat layer. Place 2 pickle spears on top of each other near one edge of the meat (where you will start the roll). Starting at the pickle end, roll up the meat as tightly as possible and secure it with toothpicks or cooking twine. Make sure to roll them up with the grain running lengthwise, so that when you cut the meat, you will cut against the grain.

3. Add 2 tablespoons (29 g) of healthy fat of choice to the Instant Pot and press "Sauté." Add the beef rolls and brown for about 5 minutes per side (you will need to do this in two batches). Remove the browned beef rolls to a plate and set aside. When all the beef rolls are browned, transfer them back in the Instant Pot and add the beef bone broth or pickle juice and the remaining ½ teaspoon of salt. Place the lid on the Instant Pot, making sure the steam release valve is sealed. Press the "Meat/Stew" setting for 35 minutes.

4. When the Instant Pot is done and beeps, press "Keep Warm/Cancel." Using an oven mitt, "quick release"/open the steam release valve. When the steam venting stops and the silver dial drops, carefully open the lid. Remove the beef rolls, plate them and set aside.

5. Turn the Instant Pot on by pressing "Sauté." Sprinkle 2 tablespoons (26 g) flour of choice over the surface of the beef broth or mix 1 tablespoon (8 g) of cornstarch and 1 tablespoon (15 ml) of water in a small bowl, then pour into the beef broth, whisking constantly until the gravy thickens, about 5 to 7 minutes. Press "Keep Warm/Cancel."

6. Plate the rouladen, remove cooking twine or toothpicks, ladle gravy over the top and garnish with fresh chopped Italian parsley. Serve immediately.

Ginger Beef Tips with Bone Broth Gravy

Spicy yet mild, ginger is the perfect addition to tender, fall-apart, melt-in-your-mouth beef tips. The secret ingredient in the super-flavorful gravy might surprise you.

PREP TIME: 15 MINUTES | COOK TIME: 30 MINUTES | TOTAL TIME: 45 MINUTES | YIELD: 4 SERVINGS

3 tbsp (43 g) grass-fed butter, ghee or avocado oil, divided

2 small yellow onions, diced

1 large celery root, discard outer peel, diced

4 fresh garlic cloves, grated or finely minced

2½" (6-cm) knob fresh ginger, grated or finely minced

2 lbs (907 g) grass-fed beef tips or stew meat cut into 1" (2.5-cm) cubes

¾ cup (177 ml) chicken bone broth, divided

7 medium carrots, chopped into large 2" (5-cm) pieces

7 fresh thyme sprigs

⅓ cup (79 ml) coconut aminos or gluten-free tamari

1 tbsp (21 g) honey

¾ tsp sea salt

1. Press "Sauté" and add 2 tablespoons (29 g) of healthy fat of choice to the Instant Pot. When it's melted, add the onions, celery root, garlic and ginger and sauté for 5 minutes. Remove the vegetables from the Instant Pot and set aside. Add 1 tablespoon (14 g) of healthy fat of choice to the Instant Pot, then add the beef tips. Stir frequently and allow to brown for about 4 minutes.

2. While the beef tips are browning, pour the sautéed onion-celery root mixture into a blender with ¼ cup (59 ml) bone broth. Puree until smooth, about 30 seconds, then set aside.

3. Add the remaining bone broth to the Instant Pot, using a wooden spoon to scrape up the brown bits from the bottom of the pan. Add the carrots, thyme, coconut aminos, honey, sea salt and pureed onion-celery root mixture, and stir to combine. Press "Keep Warm/Cancel." Place the lid on the Instant Pot, making sure the steam release valve is sealed. Press "Meat/Stew" and decrease the cooking time using the "-" button until you reach 20 minutes.

4. When the Instant Pot is done and beeps, press "Keep Warm/Cancel," and allow the Instant Pot to release pressure naturally (this takes about 15 minutes). When the silver dial drops, carefully open the lid with an oven mitt.

5. Plate the beef tips and gravy and serve immediately.

NOTES

Celery root is the secret ingredient in this recipe. It adds a lovely bold flavor to the gravy and acts as a thickener. Celery root, also known as celeriac, is easy to find at natural food stores, most local grocers, some larger farmers markets and Asian markets. If you can't find celery root or don't care for the mild celery flavor, you can substitute with turnips, but they will change the flavor.

This dish is delicious served on top of creamy polenta (as shown in the opposite image), steamed rice or buttered noodles.

Elegant Poultry

I think most people can agree that they enjoy eating a perfectly cooked piece of chicken, and in this chapter we explore the range (pun intended!) of just how marvelous this fantastic bird can really taste. But chicken can be a temperamental food to cook. A few minutes too long and it's dry. Undercook it and it's not suitable to eat. The Instant Pot assumes its place at the top of the "pecking order" of chicken cooking, ensuring that your chicken is juicy and tender every single time.

In our home, we eat chicken 3 or 4 nights a week. It's the "go to" answer when my husband and I ask, "What's for dinner?" The Instant Pot helps us produce quick, healthy, delicious chicken dinners in a matter of minutes. How else can you make stellar dishes like Italian Chicken Cacciatore (page 46), Tomatillo-Cilantro Chicken (page 42) and Citrus-Herb Basque Chicken (page 45) in such a short amount of time? The answer is right here in this chapter.

Tomatillo-Cilantro Chicken

Tomatillos, cilantro and lime are signature Mexican flavors. Tangy, refreshing and vibrant, the combination of these flavors is a favorite in my home. Because it's so easy to make, this sweet and mildly spicy chicken dish makes an appearance on our dinner table quite often.

PREP TIME: 20 MINUTES | COOK TIME: 23 MINUTES | TOTAL TIME: 43 MINUTES | YIELD: 4 SERVINGS

4 tbsp (57 g) grass-fed butter, ghee or avocado oil

5 fresh garlic cloves, minced

6 green onions, white and light green parts only, diced

2 jalapeños, seeded and diced

1 tsp sea salt, divided

2 chicken breasts, diced

11 tomatillos, outer shell discarded, quartered

1 tsp ground cumin

Juice and zest of 1 lime, plus more for garnish

1 cup (16 g) fresh cilantro, chopped, plus more for garnish

1 cup (237 ml) chicken bone broth

1. Add healthy fat of choice to the Instant Pot and press "Sauté." Once the fat has melted, add the garlic, green onion, jalapeños and ½ teaspoon of the sea salt and sauté for 5 minutes, stirring occasionally. Add the chicken breasts and cook for about 3 minutes, stirring occasionally until no longer pink. Add the tomatillos, cumin, lime juice, lime zest, cilantro, bone broth and remaining ½ teaspoon sea salt. Give it a good stir. Press the "Keep Warm/Cancel" button. Place the lid on the Instant Pot, making sure the steam release valve is sealed. Press "Poultry" for 15 minutes.

2. When the Instant Pot is done and beeps, press "Keep Warm/Cancel." Using an oven mitt, "quick release"/open the steam release valve. When the steam venting stops and the silver dial drops, carefully open the lid.

3. Serve immediately, topped with fresh cilantro and a squeeze of fresh lime juice.

NOTE

My family loves this on top of steamed rice with veggies on the side. For a more relaxed meal, we serve this as the base for tacos.

Citrus-Herb Basque Chicken

My husband has Basque heritage. We love the simple yet bold flavors of Basque cuisine. This delightful dish is full of spicy chorizo, sun-dried tomatoes, sweet and tangy orange juice, floral thyme and salty olives. It's meant to be shared family-style with those you love.

PREP TIME: 20 MINUTES | COOK TIME: 35 MINUTES | TOTAL TIME: 55 MINUTES | YIELD: 4 SERVINGS

3 tbsp (43 g) grass-fed butter, ghee or avocado oil, divided

4 bone-in chicken thighs

1¼ tsp (4 g) sea salt, divided

1 medium yellow onion, thickly sliced

4 fresh garlic cloves, minced

5 fresh thyme sprigs, leaves removed and stems discarded

½ lb (230 g) chorizo, casing removed

⅓ cup (18 g) sun-dried tomatoes

½ cup (67 g) pitted green olives

⅓ cup (79 ml) freshly squeezed orange juice

¾ cup (177 ml) chicken bone broth

Handful of fresh cilantro, for garnish

1. Add 2 tablespoons (29 g) of healthy fat of choice to the Instant Pot and press "Sauté." Once the fat has melted, add the chicken thighs, sprinkle with ½ teaspoon of sea salt and brown for about 2½ minutes per side. Remove the browned chicken to a plate and set aside. Add the remaining 1 tablespoon (14 g) of healthy fat of choice, onion, garlic, thyme leaves and the remaining ¾ teaspoon of sea salt, sautéing for 5 minutes, stirring occasionally. Add the chorizo and sauté for 5 minutes, stirring occasionally. Press the "Keep Warm/Cancel" button. Add the sun-dried tomatoes, olives, orange juice and bone broth. Give it a good stir. Add the browned chicken, making sure it's submerged and some of the liquid is ladled over it. Place the lid on the Instant Pot, making sure the steam release valve is sealed. Press the "Poultry" setting, then increase the time using the "+" button until you reach 20 minutes.

2. When the Instant Pot is done and beeps, press "Keep Warm/Cancel." Using an oven mitt, "quick release"/open the steam release valve. When the steam venting stops and the silver dial drops, carefully open the lid.

3. Serve immediately, topped with fresh cilantro.

> **NOTE**
> This meal is delicious served alongside simple roasted vegetables.

Italian Chicken Cacciatore

Chicken cacciatore reminds me of the delicious aroma always coming from my Italian neighbors' home when I was a child. This classic "hunter-style" Italian meal has lots of browned chicken, aromatic vegetables, fragrant herbs, sweet tomatoes and salty olives and capers. It's a comforting, hearty dish and a favorite of my husband.

PREP TIME: 25 MINUTES | COOK TIME: 34 MINUTES | TOTAL TIME: 59 MINUTES | YIELD: 6 SERVINGS

3 tbsp (43 g) grass-fed butter, ghee or avocado oil, divided

3 lbs (1.4 kg) chicken thighs and legs

1¼ tsp (4 g) sea salt, divided

1 yellow onion, diced

6 fresh garlic cloves, minced

8 oz (227 g) button mushrooms, thickly sliced

2 tbsp (10 g) finely minced fresh Italian parsley

2 tsp (2 g) finely minced fresh thyme leaves

3 carrots, peeled and cut into large 2" (5-cm) pieces

9 oz (255 g) crushed or diced tomatoes

5 oz (142 g) pitted green olives

¼ cup (34 g) capers

1 cup (237 ml) chicken bone broth

¼ cup (15 g) roughly chopped fresh Italian parsley, for garnish

1. Add 2 tablespoons (29 g) of healthy fat of choice to the Instant Pot and press "Sauté." Once the fat has melted, add the chicken thighs and legs, sprinkle with ¼ teaspoon of sea salt and brown for about 2½ minutes per side. (You might have to do this in two batches depending on how much chicken you have and the size of your Instant Pot.) Remove the browned chicken, transfer to a plate and set aside.

2. Add the remaining 1 tablespoon (14 g) of healthy fat of choice, onion, garlic and the remaining 1 teaspoon of sea salt, sautéing for 7 minutes, stirring occasionally. Add the mushrooms, parsley and thyme and continue to sauté for 2 minutes, giving the mixture a good stir. Press the "Keep Warm/Cancel" button. Add the carrots, tomatoes, olives, capers and bone broth and stir to combine. Add the browned chicken pieces, making sure they're submerged and some of the liquid is ladled over them. Place the lid on the Instant Pot, making sure the steam release valve is sealed. Press the "Poultry" setting, then increase the time using the "+" button until you reach 20 minutes.

3. When the Instant Pot is done and beeps, press "Keep Warm/Cancel." Using an oven mitt, "quick release"/open the steam release valve. When the steam venting stops and the silver dial drops, carefully open the lid.

4. Serve immediately, garnished with fresh Italian parsley.

NOTES

For a different flavor and texture, use shiitake mushrooms in place of the button mushrooms, or a combination of both.

This dish is delicious paired with buttered pasta, polenta or crusty bread.

Cacao-Tomatillo Mole

My husband grew up eating mole, a traditional Mexican dish. This recipe is an homage to him. With layers of flavors from tangy tomatillos to sweet raisins to bittersweet cacao, this authentic-tasting mole is sure to please.

INACTIVE PREP TIME: 15 MINUTES | PREP TIME: 25 MINUTES | COOK TIME: 35 MINUTES | TOTAL TIME: 60 MINUTES | YIELD: 4–6 SERVINGS

3 dried New Mexico chilis

2 dried ancho chilis

4 tbsp (57 g) grass-fed butter, ghee or avocado oil

2 chicken leg quarters

1¾ tsp (5 g) sea salt, divided

1 yellow onion, diced

5 fresh garlic cloves, minced

5 fresh thyme sprigs, leaves removed and stems discarded

1 tsp cumin

½ tsp ground cinnamon

¼ tsp ground cloves

¼ cup (22 g) cacao powder

5 tomatillos, outer shell removed, quartered

2 whole peeled tomatoes, diced

½ cup (73 g) raisins, plus more for garnish

¾ cup (177 ml) freshly squeezed orange juice

¼ cup (59 ml) chicken bone broth

¼ cup (59 ml) reserved dried pepper soak water

3 tbsp (48 g) natural peanut butter, no added sugar or oil

Fresh cilantro, chopped, for garnish

Thinly sliced radishes, for garnish

1. Place the dried chilis in a glass bowl and pour just enough water over them to cover. Let them soak for 15 minutes prior to cooking. Once they've softened a bit, remove them from the water, reserving ¼ cup (59 ml) of the soaking water. Remove the stems and seeds and discard, then roughly dice the peppers. Set aside.

2. Add healthy fat of choice to the Instant Pot and press "Sauté." Once the fat has melted, add the chicken, sprinkle with ¾ teaspoon of sea salt and brown for about 2½ minutes per side. Remove the browned chicken to a plate and set aside. Add the onion, garlic, thyme leaves, cumin, cinnamon, cloves and ½ teaspoon of the sea salt, sautéing for 5 minutes, stirring occasionally. Press the "Keep Warm/Cancel" button. Add the cacao powder and stir it all around until it's fully incorporated. Add the tomatillos, tomatoes, raisins and the remaining 1 teaspoon of sea salt and give it a quick stir. To a mixing bowl or 2-cup (0.5 L) measuring cup, add the orange juice, bone broth, dried pepper soak water and peanut butter and stir until the peanut butter is mostly incorporated. Pour the peanut butter liquid into the Instant Pot and stir again to combine.

3. In batches, ladle the mole sauce into a blender, taking care to fill only about half of the blender (hot liquids will expand in the blender, so use caution). Blend on a low setting until just puréed and smooth. Transfer the mole sauce back to the Instant Pot. Add the browned chicken and spoon the mole sauce over the top until the chicken is submerged. Place the lid on the Instant Pot, making sure the steam release valve is sealed. Press the "Poultry" setting and increase the time using the "+" button until you reach 25 minutes.

4. When the Instant Pot is done and beeps, press "Keep Warm/Cancel." Using an oven mitt, "quick release"/open the steam release valve. When the steam venting stops and the silver dial drops, carefully open the lid.

5. Remove the chicken and plate on a serving dish.

6. Serve the chicken immediately with mole sauce poured over the top. Garnish with fresh cilantro, thinly sliced radishes and raisins.

Apple Cider Vinegar-Braised Chicken

This apple cider vinegar "braised" chicken is sweet, tart and tangy with caramelized leeks and apples in a mild cider-mustard sauce. This dish cooks in under 30 minutes in the Instant Pot and produces succulent chicken every time.

PREP TIME: 20 MINUTES | COOK TIME: 27 MINUTES | TOTAL TIME: 47 MINUTES | YIELD: 4–6 SERVINGS

3 tbsp (43 g) grass-fed butter, ghee or avocado oil, divided

6 chicken legs

1½ tsp (4 g) sea salt, divided

1 leek, sliced, white and light green parts only

4 fresh garlic cloves, minced

5 fresh thyme sprigs, leaves removed and stems discarded

3 apples, cored and quartered

3 tbsp (44 ml) apple cider vinegar

¾ cup (177 ml) fresh apple cider

1 tbsp (16 g) Dijon or stone-ground mustard

1. Add 2 tablespoons (29 g) of healthy fat of choice to the Instant Pot and press "Sauté." Once the fat has melted, add the chicken legs, sprinkle with ½ teaspoon of the sea salt and brown for about 2½ minutes per side. Remove the browned chicken to a plate and set aside. Add the remaining 1 tablespoon (14 g) of healthy fat of choice, leeks, garlic, thyme and the remaining 1 teaspoon of sea salt, sautéing for 7 minutes, stirring occasionally. Press the "Keep Warm/Cancel" button. Add the apples, apple cider vinegar, apple cider and mustard. Give it a good stir. Add the browned chicken legs, making sure they're submerged and some of the liquid is ladled over them. Place the lid on the Instant Pot, making sure the steam release valve is sealed. Press the "Poultry" setting for 15 minutes.

2. When the Instant Pot is done and beeps, press "Keep Warm/Cancel." Using an oven mitt, "quick release"/open the steam release valve. When the steam venting stops and the silver dial drops, carefully open the lid.

3. Serve immediately with plenty of leeks and apples.

> **NOTE**
> If you can't find fresh apple cider, use fresh apple juice. Add ⅛ teaspoon of ground cinnamon, a pinch of ground cloves, a pinch of allspice and a pinch of freshly grated nutmeg to the Instant Pot when you add the juice.

Jamaican Sweet Jerk-Spiced Chicken Legs

My husband loves his food hot and spicy, and I love to make foods he enjoys. This jerk chicken is fragrant, sweet and perfectly spiced, and it packs some heat. It's sure to please heat-lovers, but it can be made milder, too.

PREP TIME: 20 MINUTES | COOK TIME: 34 MINUTES | TOTAL TIME: 54 MINUTES | YIELD: 6 SERVINGS

3 tbsp (43 g) grass-fed butter, ghee or avocado oil, divided

8 chicken legs

1¼ tsp (4 g) sea salt, divided

1 red onion, thickly sliced

4 fresh garlic cloves, minced

2 tsp (1 g) fresh thyme leaves

1 tsp ground cinnamon

½ tsp ground cloves

½ tsp ground allspice

3 small shishito peppers or small jalapeños, seeded and diced

3 tbsp (44 ml) maple syrup, honey or maple sugar

¼ tsp crushed red pepper flakes

1 cup (237 ml) chicken bone broth

¼ cup (4 g) roughly chopped fresh cilantro, for garnish

1. Add 2 tablespoons (29 g) of healthy fat of choice to the Instant Pot and press "Sauté." Once the fat has melted, add the chicken legs, sprinkle with ¼ teaspoon of sea salt and brown for about 2½ minutes per side. Remove the browned chicken to a plate and set aside. Add the remaining 1 tablespoon (14 g) of healthy fat of choice, onion, garlic, thyme, cinnamon, cloves, allspice and the remaining 1 teaspoon of sea salt, sautéing for 7 minutes, stirring occasionally. Add the peppers and continue to sauté for 2 minutes, giving it a good stir. Press the "Keep Warm/Cancel" button. Add the sweetener of choice, red pepper flakes and bone broth and stir to combine. Add the browned chicken legs, making sure they're submerged and some of the liquid is ladled over them. Place the lid on the Instant Pot, making sure the steam release valve is sealed. Press the "Poultry" setting, then increase the time using the "+" button until you reach 20 minutes.

2. When the Instant Pot is done and beeps, press "Keep Warm/Cancel." Using an oven mitt, "quick release"/open the steam release valve. When the steam venting stops and the silver dial drops, carefully open the lid.

3. Serve immediately, garnished with some fresh cilantro.

NOTES

If you prefer to make this milder, I recommend using just one fresh pepper and omitting the red pepper flakes. If you prefer lots of heat, don't remove the seeds from the peppers. I do not recommend using the seeds if you prefer milder foods.

This meal is delicious served with rice, beans and fresh pineapple.

Spiced Lemongrass-Coconut Chicken Curry

There's something about a bowl of curry that warms the soul. With subtle hints of lemongrass, cardamom and cinnamon, the delicate flavors of this curry take you on a trip around the world.

PREP TIME: 20 MINUTES | COOK TIME: 23 MINUTES | TOTAL TIME: 43 MINUTES | YIELD: 4 SERVINGS

3 tbsp (43 g) grass-fed butter, ghee or avocado oil

4 fresh garlic cloves, minced

1 medium red onion, cut in rough dice or thickly sliced

2 tsp (4 g) mild yellow curry powder blend

¼ tsp ground cardamom

1 cinnamon stick

5" (13-cm) lemongrass stem, ends removed and halved

1¼ tsp (4 g) sea salt, divided

2 chicken breasts, cut into strips

1 large cauliflower, cut into small florets

5 carrots, peeled and cut into 2" (5-cm) pieces

13½ oz (399 ml) full-fat coconut milk

1 cup (237 ml) chicken bone broth

Handful of fresh cilantro, for garnish

1. Add healthy fat of choice to the Instant Pot and press "Sauté." Once the fat has melted, add the garlic, onion, curry powder, cardamom, cinnamon stick, lemongrass and ½ teaspoon of the sea salt and sauté for 5 minutes, stirring occasionally. Add the chicken and cook for about 3 minutes, stirring occasionally until it is no longer pink. Add the cauliflower florets, carrots, coconut milk, bone broth and the remaining ¾ teaspoon sea salt. Give it a good stir. Press the "Keep Warm/Cancel" button. Place the lid on the Instant Pot, making sure the steam release valve is sealed. Press the "Poultry" setting for 15 minutes.

2. When the Instant Pot is done and beeps, press "Keep Warm/Cancel." Using an oven mitt, "quick release"/open the steam release valve. When the steam venting stops and the silver dial drops, carefully open the lid.

3. Serve immediately, topped with fresh cilantro.

NOTES

The mild curry powder blend that I use contains coriander, turmeric, mustard, cumin, fenugreek, paprika, cayenne, cardamom, nutmeg, cinnamon and cloves. Look for a blend that uses most of these ingredients for the best flavor.

My family loves to eat this over steamed rice.

Vietnamese Lemongrass-Lime Chicken Wings

Everyone loves a good meal of chicken wings! Wings are usually served with hot sauce, creamy dipping sauce and crudités, but these Vietnamese wings are not your average hot wings. Bursting with flavor, these mouthwatering wings are braised in a garlic, ginger, lemongrass and lime sauce that is sweet and tangy.

**INACTIVE PREP TIME: 20 MINUTES | PREP TIME: 25 MINUTES | COOK TIME: 21 MINUTES |
TOTAL TIME: 46 MINUTES | YIELD: 4–6 SERVINGS**

MARINADE

¼ cup (59 ml) coconut aminos or gluten-free tamari

2 tbsp (30 ml) apple cider vinegar

1 tbsp (21 g) honey, maple syrup or maple sugar

½ tsp sea salt

CHICKEN WINGS

3 lbs (1.4 kg) chicken wings

2 tbsp (29 g) grass-fed butter or ghee

4 fresh garlic cloves, finely minced

1" (3-cm) knob fresh ginger, peeled and finely minced or grated

1 full length stem of lemongrass, cut in half lengthwise and quartered

½ tsp sea salt

2 tbsp (43 g) honey

Juice and zest of 1 lime

½ cup (118 ml) coconut water

¼ cup (59 ml) apple cider vinegar

¼ cup (59 ml) coconut aminos or gluten-free tamari

1. In a very large mixing bowl, combine all marinade ingredients and add the chicken wings. Allow to marinate for 20 minutes.

2. Add the butter to the Instant Pot and press "Sauté." Once the fat has melted, add the garlic, ginger, lemongrass and sea salt, sautéing for 5 minutes, stirring occasionally. Add the honey and lime juice to deglaze the pan, then add the lime zest, coconut water, apple cider vinegar and aminos, and give it a good stir. Gently add the chicken wings into the liquid mixture. Place the lid on the Instant Pot, making sure the steam release valve is sealed. Press the "Poultry" setting, then decrease the time with the "-" button until you reach 13 minutes.

3. When the Instant Pot is done and beeps, press "Keep Warm/Cancel." Allow to release pressure naturally for 15 minutes. While the Instant Pot is naturally releasing pressure, get a baking sheet ready and preheat your broiler.

4. Using an oven mitt, "quick release"/open the steam release valve. When the steam venting stops and the silver dial drops, carefully open the lid.

5. Carefully transfer the chicken wings to the baking sheet and place under the middle rack broiler for 1 to 3 minutes, to lightly brown (do not walk away because you do not want these to burn). Flip over the wings and repeat.

6. Serve immediately with the cooking liquid for dipping.

NOTES

For a thicker sauce, add a cornstarch slurry to the sauce after the wings have been cooked and removed from the Instant Pot. Combine 1 tablespoon (8 g) of cornstarch with 1 tablespoon (15 ml) cold water, mix until uniform, then whisk that into the sauce, heating until thickened.

For a special touch, serve these with an Asian vinaigrette and mixed greens salad, topped with steamed buttered jasmine rice (cooked in bone broth or coconut milk and studded with chopped cilantro or mint), with the chicken wings layered on top.

Tomatillo Chicken Tamales

Mexican tamales, traditionally steamed in corn husks or plantain/banana leaves, are always a crowd-pleaser. These tamales are filled with very moist corn masa and saucy tomatillo shredded chicken and studded with bites of salty pimento-stuffed green olives. I have found that it's much more efficient to cook tamales in the Instant Pot than any other way.

PREP TIME: 60 MINUTES | COOK TIME: 20 MINUTES | TOTAL TIME: 80 MINUTES | YIELD: 20 TAMALES

20 corn husks

1 recipe Tomatillo-Cilantro Chicken (page 42)

1½ cups (183 g) masa harina

½ cup (115 g) grass-fed butter or lard, softened

1 tsp baking powder

½ tsp sea salt

1 cup (237 ml) chicken bone broth

15 pimento green olives, sliced

1. Rinse the corn husks, place them in a large dish and cover them with very hot water, making sure they are fully submerged. Set aside.

2. Make the filling using Tomatillo-Cilantro Chicken (page 42).

3. Make the masa. In a standing mixer bowl, add the masa harina, butter or lard, baking powder and sea salt. With the mixer on low, very slowly add the bone broth and mix until the dough becomes soft and sticky.

4. Create a flat work space area on your counter or table and line up all the tamale ingredients—the husks, masa, filling and sliced olives. Set a clean kitchen towel by your work space. Flip the corn husks over so the one that soaked on the bottom is now on the top and ready to use. Using the towel, wipe off the excess moisture on 5 corn husks, then place them on your flat work surface. Spread a layer of masa about ¼" (6 mm) thick in the middle top of each corn husk. Add about 2 tablespoons (29 g) of the filling to the middle of the masa. Add 3 to 5 olive slices to each filling. Gently fold up the corn husks, folding the sides of the husks toward the center, then fold the bottom later of the husk up, leaving the top open. Repeat until all tamales are filled.

5. Place a steamer basket in the Instant Pot. Pour 2 cups (473 ml) of water into the Instant Pot. Add as many tamales as you can to the Instant Pot, letting them stand vertically, not horizontally. Go ahead and stuff them in there. Place the lid on the Instant Pot, making sure the steam release valve is sealed. Press the "Steam" setting and increase the time using the "+" button until you reach 20 minutes.

6. When the Instant Pot is done and beeps, press "Keep Warm/Cancel." Allow it to release pressure naturally for 10 minutes. Using an oven mitt, "quick release"/open the steam release valve. When the steam venting stops and the silver dial drops, carefully open the lid.

7. Serve the hot tamales in their wrappers.

> **NOTE**
> You can find corn husks and masa harina at most grocery stores, or you can purchase them online.

Preserved Lemon-Turmeric Chicken

The slightly bitter and aromatic flavor of turmeric pairs perfectly with tart lemons and salty olives in this golden, brothy dish. It's full of nourishing, immune-supporting ingredients such as ginger, turmeric, garlic, onions and preserved lemons.

PREP TIME: 20 MINUTES | COOK TIME: 27 MINUTES | TOTAL TIME: 47 MINUTES | YIELD: 4–6 SERVINGS

3 tbsp (43 g) grass-fed butter, ghee or avocado oil, divided

6 chicken legs

1½ tsp (4 g) sea salt, divided

1 medium red onion, thickly sliced

6 fresh garlic cloves, minced

1" (3-cm) knob fresh ginger, peeled and finely minced or grated

½ tsp ground turmeric powder

1 tbsp (21 g) honey

1 tbsp (15 ml) apple cider vinegar

¼ cup (59 ml) fresh lemon juice

¾ cup (177 ml) chicken bone broth

½ cup (67 g) pitted green olives

½ cup (72 g) sliced preserved or fermented lemons

1. Add 2 tablespoons (29 g) of healthy fat of choice to the Instant Pot and press "Sauté." Once the fat has melted, add the chicken legs, sprinkle with ½ teaspoon of the sea salt and brown for about 2½ minutes per side. Remove the browned chicken to a plate and set aside. Add the remaining 1 tablespoon (14 g) of healthy fat of choice, onion, garlic, ginger, turmeric and the remaining 1 teaspoon of sea salt, sautéing for 7 minutes, stirring occasionally. Press the "Keep Warm/Cancel" button. Add the honey, apple cider vinegar, lemon juice, bone broth, olives and preserved lemons. Give it a good stir. Add the browned chicken legs, making sure they're submerged and some of the liquid is ladled over them. Place the lid on the Instant Pot, making sure the steam release valve is sealed. Press the "Poultry" setting for 15 minutes.

2. When the Instant Pot is done and beeps, press "Keep Warm/Cancel." Using an oven mitt, "quick release"/open the steam release valve. When the steam venting stops and the silver dial drops, carefully open the lid.

3. Serve immediately.

NOTE
Preserved lemons and fermented lemons are easy to find at most natural food stores. If you're not able to find any, you can substitute fresh lemons, preferably Meyer lemons.

Delectable Pastas, Seafood, Vegetables & More

No matter what the season, there are certain meals that you can eat all the time and never get tired of. For me, pastas, seafood and veggie dishes never get old.

Pasta is always a crowd-pleaser. My family loves pasta meals. There's something magic about grating fresh parmesan over a big plate of steaming Bacon, Kale & Mushroom Spaghetti (page 64) and watching little eyes get big.

When I think of the best fine dining experiences I've had, seafood always comes to mind. Seafood is the one food group that is almost exclusively gourmet without any other additional ingredients.

The Instant Pot brings all these foods together in perfect harmony and cooks them beautifully. In this chapter, you will find exquisite recipes such as Lemon-Mornay Garlicky Spinach & Shrimp Penne (page 67), Caramelized Mushroom & Onion Crustless Quiche (page 71) and Valencian Bone Broth Paella (page 76).

Bacon, Kale & Mushroom Spaghetti

There's nothing as comforting as a big plate of spaghetti. This quick pasta dish is full of garlicky caramelized onions and mushrooms, good-for-you kale, hints of zesty lemon and salty, crispy bacon. It's some seriously soul-soothing comfort food.

PREP TIME: 25 MINUTES | COOK TIME: 31 MINUTES | TOTAL TIME: 56 MINUTES | YIELD: 6 SERVINGS

8 oz (227 g) pastured bacon, diced

4 tbsp (57 g) grass-fed butter

1 red or yellow onion, sliced

4 fresh garlic cloves, finely minced

8 oz (227 g) white or cremini mushrooms, sliced

½ lb (230 g) kale, de-ribbed and thinly sliced

Zest of 1 lemon

1 cup (237 ml) chicken bone broth

3 cups (710 ml) water

12 oz (340 g) spaghetti, broken in half

1 tsp sea salt

½ cup (50 g) grated raw parmigiano-reggiano

1. Press "Sauté" and add the bacon to the Instant Pot. Cook, stirring occasionally, until the bacon is crispy, about 10 to 15 minutes. Turn off the Instant Pot by pressing "Keep Warm/Cancel," remove the crispy bacon and set aside. Pour the bacon grease out of the Instant Pot and discard. Don't worry about washing the Instant Pot; a little leftover bacon grease is fine.

2. Add the butter to the Instant Pot and press "Sauté." Once the fat has melted, add the onion and garlic and sauté for 5 minutes until translucent. Add the mushrooms and continue to sauté for 5 minutes until they start to turn golden brown. Turn off the Instant Pot by pressing "Keep Warm/Cancel." Add the kale and lemon zest and give a couple of stirs. Add the broth, water, spaghetti, half of the reserved crispy bacon and salt and give it one more stir. Place the lid on the Instant Pot, making sure the steam release valve is sealed. Press "Manual" and decrease the cooking time by using the "-" button until you reach 6 minutes.

3. When the Instant Pot is done and beeps, press "Keep Warm/Cancel." Allow it to release pressure naturally for 5 minutes. When the 5 minutes are up, unplug the Instant Pot and use an oven mitt to "quick release"/open the steam release valve. When the steam venting stops and the silver dial drops, carefully open the lid. Give the spaghetti a gentle stir to combine.

4. Serve immediately, topped with the remaining crispy bacon and grated parmigiano-reggiano cheese.

> **NOTE**
> If you prefer, the bacon can be cooked in a skillet or baked in the oven (instead of the Instant Pot) until crispy. You can crumble up the bacon into small pieces, roughly chop it or serve it in full strips with the pasta.

Lemon-Mornay Garlicky Spinach & Shrimp Penne

There's nothing more decadent than creamy French Mornay sauce. This swoon-worthy sauce is enlivened by refreshing, vibrant lemon juice. Garlicky spinach, shrimp and pasta get drenched in this glorious sauce and make for one truly satisfying meal.

PREP TIME: 15 MINUTES | COOK TIME: 7 MINUTES | TOTAL TIME: 22 MINUTES | YIELD: 6 SERVINGS

3 tbsp (43 g) grass-fed butter, ghee or avocado oil

5 fresh garlic cloves, minced

2½ cups (592 ml) milk

1 cup (237 ml) filtered water

12 oz (340 g) penne pasta

1½ tsp (4 g) sea salt

16 wild-caught shrimp, deveined and peeled

3 oz (85 g) spinach

¼ cup (59 ml) cream

2 oz (57 g) gruyère cheese, shredded

Juice and zest of 1 lemon

¼ cup (15 g) fresh Italian parsley, chopped

1. Add healthy fat of choice to the Instant Pot and press "Sauté." Once the fat has melted, add the garlic, sautéing for 2 minutes, stirring occasionally. Press the "Keep Warm/Cancel" button.

2. Add the milk, water, pasta, salt, shrimp and spinach to the Instant Pot and give it a gentle stir. Place the lid on the Instant Pot, making sure the steam release valve is sealed. Press the "Manual" setting for 5 minutes.

3. When the Instant Pot is done and beeps, press "Keep Warm/Cancel." Using an oven mitt, "quick release"/open the steam release valve. When the steam venting stops and the silver dial drops, carefully open the lid.

4. Add the cream and shredded cheese and give the pasta a stir to combine. Add the lemon juice and zest and continue stirring until fully combined. Allow the pasta to sit in the Instant Pot for 5 minutes while the creamy sauce thickens up a bit.

5. Serve immediately and garnish with fresh chopped parsley.

> **NOTE**
> I use gluten-free brown rice penne pasta in this dish, but any dry pasta will work.

Pumpkin & Sage-Stuffed Manicotti

One of my favorite gourmet restaurant pasta dishes growing up was a pumpkin-stuffed pasta with crispy fried sage leaves. The flavor was heavenly! This stuffed manicotti is my re-creation of my favorite pasta in the Instant Pot. The tube-shaped noodles are filled with cheesy pumpkin-sage goodness and showered with a delectable garlic cream sauce. True bliss!

PREP TIME: 30 MINUTES | COOK TIME: 34 MINUTES | TOTAL TIME: 64 MINUTES | YIELD: 4–6 SERVINGS

CREAM SAUCE

2 tbsp (29 g) grass-fed butter, ghee or avocado oil

4 fresh garlic cloves, minced

1 tsp dried thyme

½ tsp sea salt

1 tbsp (8 g) all-purpose gluten-free flour, cassava flour or other all-purpose flour

1½ cups (355 ml) cream

MANICOTTI

1½ cups (170 g) shredded cheddar cheese

½ cup (57 g) shredded mozzarella

¼ cup (20 g) shredded parmigiano-reggiano

1 cup (245 g) pumpkin purée

1 cup (246 g) ricotta cheese

1 pastured egg, lightly beaten

1 tsp fresh sage leaves, finely chopped

1 tsp sea salt

7 oz (199 g) manicotti shells (1 package), parboiled for 4 minutes

1 cup (237 ml) water

1. Make the cream sauce before you fill the manicotti shells. To a medium saucepan, add 2 tablespoons (29 g) of healthy fat choice over medium heat. Once the fat has melted, add the garlic, thyme and ½ teaspoon sea salt, stirring occasionally for 2 minutes until fragrant. Add 1 tablespoon (8 g) of flour of choice and stir quickly until combined. Add the cream and bring to a simmer, stirring occasionally until the sauce thickens, about 5 minutes. Set aside.

2. In a small bowl, combine the cheddar, mozzarella and parmigiano-reggiano.

3. In a large mixing bowl, combine the pumpkin purée, ricotta cheese, ¾ of the cheese mixture (reserving ¼ of the mixture for the top of the pasta), egg, sage and 1 teaspoon of sea salt. Stir until fully incorporated. Add the mixture to a piping bag, or use a resealable plastic bag and cut a small opening off one tip. Pipe the pumpkin filling into the pre-cooked manicotti shells. Arrange the filled manicotti shells, stacking them as you go, in a 1½-quart (1.5-L) casserole dish with a glass lid that fits inside the Instant Pot. Pour the cream sauce over the stuffed manicotti shells. Place the glass lid on top of the casserole dish. Add the trivet insert to the Instant Pot. Pour 1 cup (237 ml) of water into the Instant Pot. Set the covered casserole dish on top of the trivet. Place the lid on the Instant Pot, making sure the steam release valve is sealed. Press the "Manual" setting and decrease the time using the "-" button until you reach 22 minutes.

4. When the Instant Pot is done and beeps, press "Keep Warm/Cancel." Allow the Instant Pot to naturally release for 10 minutes. Using an oven mitt, "quick release"/ open the steam release valve. When the steam venting stops and the silver dial drops, carefully open the lid.

5. Carefully remove the casserole dish lid and sprinkle the reserved ¼ of the cheese mixture over the top of the manicotti. Next, either place the lid back on the dish for about 3 minutes to melt the cheese or carefully remove the casserole dish and place under a preheated broiler for 3 to 5 minutes until the cheese forms a golden-brown crust.

6. Serve immediately.

> **NOTE**
> I use gluten-free brown rice manicotti shells that are made in Italy, but any manicotti shells should work well in this recipe.

Caramelized Mushroom & Onion Crustless Quiche

This rich quiche is one of my favorites. It's overflowing with earthy caramelized mushrooms, sweet raisins, nutritious kale, creamy ricotta and hints of lemon.

PREP TIME: 25 MINUTES | COOK TIME: 37 MINUTES | TOTAL TIME: 62 MINUTES | YIELD: 6 SERVINGS

2 tbsp (29 g) grass-fed butter or ghee, plus some butter for greasing dish

7 button or cremini mushrooms, sliced

1 small yellow onion, diced

3 fresh garlic cloves, grated or finely minced

½ tsp dried thyme

½ lb (230 g) dinosaur (lacinato) kale, de-ribbed and chopped

6 pastured eggs

½ cup (118 g) cream

1 tsp sea salt

¼ cup (36 g) raisins

Zest of 1 lemon

½ cup (57 g) shredded aged or sharp cheddar cheese

¼ cup (62 g) ricotta cheese

1 cup (237 ml) water

1. Add the butter to the Instant Pot and press "Sauté." Once the fat has melted, add the mushrooms, onion, garlic and thyme, sautéing for 10 minutes until lightly caramelized. Add the kale and sauté for another 2 minutes just until wilted. Press the "Keep Warm/Cancel" button.

2. With butter, grease a 1½-quart (1.5-L) casserole dish (I use one with a glass lid) that fits inside the Instant Pot. Set aside. In a large mixing bowl, whisk the eggs and cream together until the eggs are fully incorporated. Add the sea salt, raisins, lemon zest, ¾ of the cheddar cheese (reserving the rest for the top) and the mushroom-kale mixture, gently stirring to fully combine. Pour the mixture into a greased casserole dish. Evenly drop little dollops of ricotta into the custard filling. Place the glass lid on top of the casserole dish. Place the Instant Pot trivet inside the Instant Pot. Pour 1 cup (237 ml) of water into the Instant Pot. Carefully transfer the covered casserole dish to the Instant Pot on top of the trivet. Place the lid on the Instant Pot, making sure the steam release valve is sealed. Press the "Manual" setting and decrease the time using the "-" button until you reach 20 minutes.

3. When the Instant Pot is done and beeps, press "Keep Warm/Cancel." Allow the Instant Pot to release pressure naturally for 10 minutes. Using an oven mitt, "quick release"/open the steam release valve. When the steam venting stops and the silver dial drops, carefully open the lid.

4. Carefully remove the casserole dish from the Instant Pot and remove the lid. Next, add the leftover cheese to the top of the quiche. Either place the Instant Pot lid back on the Instant Pot for about 3 minutes to melt the cheese or carefully remove the casserole dish and place under a preheated broiler for 3 to 5 minutes to brown the cheese on the top.

5. Serve hot or warm.

NOTE
You will need a 1½-quart (1.5-L) casserole dish or a 6-cup (1.5-L) heat-safe glass or stainless steel bowl that fits in the Instant Pot for this quiche. You will also need a lid. I use a casserole dish that comes with a glass lid. If you don't have a lid for your dish or bowl, place a piece of parchment paper over the top of the quiche, then cover it securely with foil.

Mediterranean Spinach-Feta Pie

This savory pie has the lovely flavors of spanakopita. It's loaded with nutrient-dense spinach, fragrant herbs, crumbled, creamy feta cheese and a hint of sweet nutmeg.

PREP TIME: 25 MINUTES | COOK TIME: 30 MINUTES | TOTAL TIME: 55 MINUTES | YIELD: 6 SERVINGS

2 tbsp (29 g) grass-fed butter or ghee, plus some butter for greasing dish

1 small yellow onion, diced

4 fresh garlic cloves, grated or finely minced

1½ lbs (680 g) spinach, washed, dried and chopped

3 pastured eggs

½ cup (118 ml) cream

1 tsp sea salt

Zest of 1 lemon

¼ cup (15 g) chopped fresh Italian parsley

2 tbsp (7 g) chopped fresh dill

¼ tsp nutmeg, freshly grated

½ cup (50 g) shredded parmigiano-reggiano

1½ cups (225 g) crumbled feta cheese

1 cup (237 ml) water

1. Add the butter to the Instant Pot and press "Sauté." Once the fat has melted, add the onion and garlic, sautéing for 7 minutes, until lightly caramelized. Add the spinach and sauté for another 3 minutes just until wilted. Press the "Keep Warm/Cancel" button.

2. With butter, grease a 1½-quart (1.5-L) casserole dish (I use one with a glass lid) that fits inside the Instant Pot. Set aside.

3. In a large mixing bowl, whisk together the eggs and cream until the eggs are fully incorporated. Add the sea salt, lemon zest, parsley, dill and nutmeg, gently stirring to fully combine. Add the parmigiano-reggiano cheese and the onion-garlic-spinach mixture, stirring to combine. Pour the mixture into a greased casserole dish. Evenly drop crumbles of feta into the filling. Place the glass lid on top of the casserole dish. Place the Instant Pot trivet inside the Instant Pot. Pour 1 cup (237 ml) of water into the Instant Pot. Carefully transfer the covered casserole dish to the Instant Pot on top of the trivet. Place the lid on the Instant Pot, making sure the steam release valve is sealed. Press "Manual" and decrease the time using the "-" button until you reach 20 minutes.

4. When the Instant Pot is done and beeps, press "Keep Warm/Cancel." Allow the Instant Pot to release pressure naturally for 10 minutes. Using an oven mitt, "quick release"/open the steam release valve. When the steam venting stops and the silver dial drops, carefully open the lid.

5. Carefully remove the casserole dish from the Instant Pot and remove the lid.

6. Serve hot or warm.

> **NOTE**
> You will need a 1½-quart (1.5-L) casserole dish or a 6-cup (1.5-L) heat-safe glass or stainless steel bowl that fits in the Instant Pot. You will also need a lid. I use a casserole dish that comes with a glass lid. If you don't have a lid for your dish or bowl, place a piece of parchment paper over the top, then secure it with foil.

Tarte au Pistou with Crème Fraîche

Tarte au pistou is a traditional French meal that is similar to a quiche, with a fresh garlic-tomato-basil coulis. As with all quiches, frittatas and tarts, the Instant Pot works its magic with this dish, cooking it quickly and perfectly each time.

PREP TIME: 25 MINUTES | COOK TIME: 29 MINUTES | TOTAL TIME: 54 MINUTES | YIELD: 6 SERVINGS

2 tbsp (29 g) grass-fed butter or ghee, plus some butter for greasing dish

5 fresh garlic cloves, grated or finely minced

1 cup (149 g) halved cherry tomatoes

Zest of 1 lemon

2 tsp (10 ml) fresh lemon juice

1 tsp sea salt, divided

½ cup (20 g) chopped fresh basil leaves

3 pastured eggs

7.5 oz (213 g) crème fraîche, softened

½ cup (50 g) shredded parmigiano-reggiano

1 cup (237 ml) water

1. Add the butter to the Instant Pot and press "Sauté." Once the fat has melted, add the garlic, tomatoes, lemon zest, lemon juice and ½ teaspoon of sea salt, sautéing for 5 minutes just until the tomatoes burst and soften. Add the basil and sauté for 1 minute, just until aromatic. Press the "Keep Warm/Cancel" button. Set aside.

2. With butter, grease a 1½-quart (1.5-L) casserole dish (I use one with a glass lid) that fits inside the Instant Pot. Set aside.

3. In a large mixing bowl, whisk together the eggs and crème fraîche until the eggs are fully incorporated. Pour the mixture into the greased casserole dish. Evenly pour the tomato sauce over the top, then sprinkle with parmigiano-reggiano. Place the glass lid on top of the casserole dish. Place the Instant Pot trivet inside the Instant Pot. Pour 1 cup (237 ml) of water into the Instant Pot. Carefully transfer the covered casserole dish to the Instant Pot on top of the trivet. Place the lid on the Instant Pot, making sure the steam release valve is sealed. Press "Manual" and decrease the time using the "-" button until you reach 20 minutes.

4. When the Instant Pot is done and beeps, press "Keep Warm/Cancel." Allow the Instant Pot to release pressure naturally for 10 minutes. Using an oven mitt, "quick release"/open the steam release valve. When the steam venting stops and the silver dial drops, carefully open the lid.

5. Carefully remove the casserole dish from the Instant Pot and remove the lid. Optional: Place under a preheated broiler for about 3 minutes to lightly brown the top.

6. Slice and serve hot or warm.

NOTE
You will need a 1½-quart (1.5-L) casserole dish that fits in the Instant Pot. You will also need a lid. I use a casserole dish that comes with a glass lid. If you don't have a lid for your dish or bowl, you can place a piece of parchment paper over the top, then secure it with foil.

Valencian Bone Broth Paella

This Spanish-inspired paella is similar to risotto but drier in texture. Brimming with vegetables, shellfish and browned chicken, it's a showstopper. Like all rice-based Instant Pot dishes, this paella cooks to perfection much more quickly than traditional paella.

PREP TIME: 30 MINUTES | COOK TIME: 29 MINUTES | TOTAL TIME: 59 MINUTES | YIELD: 6–8 SERVINGS

4 tbsp (57 g) grass-fed butter or ghee, divided

3–4 boneless chicken thighs

2 small shallots, sliced

4 fresh garlic cloves, minced

1 cup (200 g) Arborio or short-grain rice

1½ tsp (4 g) sea salt

Juice of 1 lemon

¼ cup (15 g) chopped fresh Italian parsley, plus more for garnish

1 lb (454 g) green beans, ends trimmed

½ cup (82 g) frozen lima beans

7 oz (198 g) artichoke hearts (not marinated)

3 oz (85 g) pimento or piquillo peppers, sliced into 2" (5-cm) pieces

1¾ cups (414 ml) fish stock or chicken bone broth

Pinch saffron (optional)

1 lb (454 g) shellfish—fresh or frozen wild-caught shrimp, mussels, clams, lobster tails, etc.

Lemon wedges

1. Add 2 tablespoons (29 g) of butter to the Instant Pot and press "Sauté." Once the fat has melted, add the chicken, browning on both sides, about 3 minutes per side. Remove the chicken and transfer to a plate, set aside. Add the remaining 2 tablespoons (29 g) of healthy fat of choice to the Instant Pot along with shallots and garlic, sautéing for 6 minutes, stirring occasionally. Once the shallots have a little light brown color, add the rice and sea salt. Give it all a stir, toasting for 2 minutes. Add the lemon juice to deglaze the Instant Pot, using a wooden spoon to scrape up any brown bits at the bottom. Add the parsley, green beans, lima beans, artichoke hearts, peppers, broth and saffron (if using), giving everything a gentle stir. Add the browned chicken and shellfish of choice. Press the "Keep Warm/Cancel" button. Place the lid on the Instant Pot, making sure the steam release valve is sealed. Press "Manual" and decrease the time using the "-" button until you reach 15 minutes.

2. When the Instant Pot is done and beeps, press "Keep Warm/Cancel." Using an oven mitt, "quick release"/open the steam release valve. When the steam venting stops and the silver dial drops, carefully open the lid.

3. Serve immediately with lemon wedges and freshly chopped Italian parsley.

> **NOTE**
> Make sure to use sustainable shellfish. If using mussels and clams, wash and scrub them well. If any of them do not open during the cooking process, discard them. Unopened shellfish are not safe to eat. If using frozen seafood, there is no need to thaw it first. One of the beautiful things about the Instant Pot is that frozen food doesn't require any extra cooking time.

Garlic-Herb Clams

Garlicky, herby clams always remind me of a childhood friend and my husband, both of whom loved linguine with clams as young children. This elegant meal is easy and quick to make in the Instant Pot.

PREP TIME: 20 MINUTES | COOK TIME: 7 MINUTES | TOTAL TIME: 27 MINUTES | YIELD: 10+ SERVINGS

2 tbsp (29 g) grass-fed butter, ghee or avocado oil

5 fresh garlic cloves, finely minced

3 tbsp (8 g) finely chopped fresh basil

3 tbsp (11 g) finely chopped fresh Italian parsley

2 cups (473 g) water

1 cup (237 g) fish stock or chicken bone broth

¼ cup (59 ml) quality dry white wine

Juice of 1 lemon

1 tsp sea salt

3 lbs (1.4 kg) fresh clams, cleaned and scrubbed

1. Add healthy fat of choice to the Instant Pot and press "Sauté." Once the fat has melted, add the garlic and sauté for 2 minutes. Add the basil and parsley, stirring to combine. Add the water, fish stock, white wine, lemon juice and sea salt and continue to cook until the liquid comes to a boil. Press "Keep Warm/Cancel." Carefully place the Instant Pot trivet inside, then add all the clams. Place the lid on the Instant Pot, making sure the steam release valve is sealed. Press "Manual" and decrease the time using the "-" button until you reach 5 minutes.

2. When the Instant Pot is done and beeps, press "Keep Warm/Cancel." Using an oven mitt, "quick release"/open the steam release valve. When the steam venting stops and the silver dial drops, carefully open the lid.

3. Discard any clams that did not open. They will not be safe to eat. Carefully transfer the clams to a serving bowl with the cooking liquid.

4. Serve as-is, garnished with freshly chopped Italian parsley or over buttered linguine pasta with freshly grated parmigiano-reggiano.

Gelatin-Rich Dill & Shrimp Risotto

This easy risotto is full of gelatin-rich bone broth and packed with sweet, aromatic dill. The bright dill flavor shines through this buttery risotto studded with wild-caught shrimp. Best of all, it cooks in only 14 minutes! There's no need to stir constantly on a hot stove when you can make risotto in half the time in the Instant Pot.

PREP TIME: 15 MINUTES | COOK TIME: 14 MINUTES | TOTAL TIME: 29 MINUTES | YIELD: 6 SERVINGS

3 tbsp (43 g) grass-fed butter or ghee, divided

4 fresh garlic cloves, minced

2 small shallots, sliced

2 cups (400 g) Arborio or short-grain rice

1½ tsp (4 g) sea salt

Juice of 1 lemon

4 cups (946 ml) chicken bone broth

16 wild-caught shrimp, peeled and deveined

⅓ cup (18 g) chopped fresh dill, plus more for garnish

1 oz (28 g) parmigiano-reggiano, shredded, plus more for garnish

1. Add 2 tablespoons (29 g) of butter to the Instant Pot and press "Sauté." Once the fat has melted, add the garlic and shallots, sautéing for 7 minutes, stirring occasionally. Once the shallots have a little light brown color, add the rice and sea salt. Give it a stir, toasting it for 2 minutes. Add lemon juice to deglaze the Instant Pot, using a wooden spoon to scrape up any brown bits at the bottom of the pot. Add the bone broth, shrimp and dill, giving everything a gentle stir. Press the "Keep Warm/Cancel" button. Place the lid on the Instant Pot, making sure the steam release valve is sealed. Press "Manual" and decrease the time with the "-" button until you reach 5 minutes.

2. When the Instant Pot is done and beeps, press "Keep Warm/Cancel." Using an oven mitt, "quick release"/open the steam release valve. When the steam venting stops and the silver dial drops, carefully open the lid.

3. Add the remaining 1 tablespoon (14 g) of butter and the shredded cheese and give the risotto a stir to combine.

4. Serve immediately and garnish with more fresh chopped dill and finely grated parmigiano-reggiano.

> **NOTE**
> This risotto is delicious served with a fluffy pillow of finely grated parmigiano-reggiano on top. To get an extra-fine grate, try using a microplane.

Beautiful Soups

Whether it's brothy, creamy, puréed or hearty, a beautiful soup is always a crowd-pleaser.

The Instant Pot makes soups as easy as 1-2-3! First, it makes nourishing broths (pages 116–123) from scratch more quickly than on the stove or in a slow cooker. Second, it locks in flavors that would ordinarily take hours of simmering and stirring. And third, it cooks meaty soups to perfection so that each bite is mouthwatering.

Soup can be enjoyed year-round. It's a universal food that all cultures have enjoyed throughout history. It brings people together, whether it's served family-style or presented in an elegant fashion. In this chapter, you will find some of my family's favorite soups, such as Italian Pappa al Pomodoro (page 84), Zucchini Soup with Crème Fraîche (page 87) and Albondigas Savory Meatball Soup with Cilantro & Mint (page 100).

Italian Pappa al Pomodoro

My mother liked an elegant Italian restaurant in the Bay Area of California. She always had their Italian pappa al pomodoro, a traditional thick Tuscan soup that's made with day-old bread, tomatoes and fresh herbs. This soup warms the soul and is a loving tribute to my mom.

PREP TIME: 30 MINUTES | COOK TIME: 40 MINUTES | TOTAL TIME: 70 MINUTES | YIELD: 8 SERVINGS

1 loaf day-old, crusty baguette or sourdough bread, crusts removed, cut into 1" (3-cm) cubes

5 tbsp (72 g) grass-fed butter or ghee, melted, divided

½ cup (50 g) freshly shredded parmigiano-reggiano

6 fresh garlic cloves, minced, divided

1 yellow onion, diced

1 small fennel bulb, tough outer stalks removed, cored and thinly sliced

3 fresh thyme sprigs, leaves removed and stems discarded

1½ tsp (4 g) sea salt, divided

¼ tsp freshly ground black pepper

28 oz (794 g) crushed tomatoes

4 cups (946 ml) chicken bone broth

¼ cup (10 g) chopped fresh basil

½ cup (118 ml) cream

3 tbsp (44 ml) good-quality extra-virgin olive oil, for garnish

1. Preheat the oven to 375°F (191°C). Spread the bread cubes over a baking sheet. Pour 3 tablespoons (43 g) of melted butter over the bread. Sprinkle with the parmigiano-reggiano and 2 minced garlic cloves. Using clean hands, toss the bread cubes until they are coated. Bake for 20 minutes, remove from the oven and set aside.

2. Add 2 tablespoons (29 g) of healthy fat of choice to the Instant Pot and press "Sauté." Once the fat has melted, add the onion, 4 cloves of minced garlic, fennel, thyme leaves, ½ teaspoon of sea salt and pepper, sautéing for 10 minutes, stirring occasionally. Press the "Keep Warm/Cancel" button. Add the crushed tomatoes, bone broth, basil and remaining 1 teaspoon of sea salt. Stir to combine. Place the lid on the Instant Pot, making sure the steam release valve is sealed. Press "Soup" and decrease the time with the "-" button until you reach 5 minutes.

3. When the Instant Pot is done and beeps, press "Keep Warm/Cancel." Using an oven mitt, "quick release"/open the steam release valve. When the steam venting stops and the silver dial drops, carefully open the lid.

4. Press "Sauté" and add the cream, stirring to combine. Add the cheesy toasted bread cubes and stir to combine. Once the soup starts to boil, allow it to continue boiling for 5 minutes. Turn off the Instant Pot by pressing "Keep Warm/Cancel."

5. Serve hot or warm, drizzled with a generous amount of extra-virgin olive oil.

> **NOTE**
> Gluten-free breads are easy to find at almost all natural food stores, as well as at some mainstream grocery stores. Crusty baguettes and sourdough are best for this soup.

Zucchini Soup with Crème Fraîche

Summer courgettes paired with creamy, herby pesto make for bliss in every bite. This is one of those soups that you will crave every day.

PREP TIME: 15 MINUTES | COOK TIME: 15 MINUTES | TOTAL TIME: 30 MINUTES | YIELD: 4 SERVINGS

4 tbsp (57 g) grass-fed butter or ghee

1 yellow onion, diced

5 fresh garlic cloves, minced

7 fresh thyme sprigs, leaves removed and stems discarded

2 tsp (6 g) sea salt, divided

4 cups (496 g) diced zucchini (about 6 zucchini)

1 cup (40 g) chopped fresh basil

4 cups (946 ml) chicken bone broth or vegetable stock

4 oz (113 g) crème fraîche or sour cream

1. Add the butter to the Instant Pot and press "Sauté." Once the fat has melted, add the onion, garlic, thyme leaves and 1 teaspoon of sea salt, sautéing for 5 minutes, stirring occasionally. Press the "Keep Warm/Cancel" button. Add the zucchini, basil, bone broth and the remaining 1 teaspoon of sea salt. Place the lid on the Instant Pot, making sure the steam release valve is sealed. Press "Soup" and decrease the time using the "-" button until you reach 10 minutes.

2. When the Instant Pot is done and beeps, press "Keep Warm/Cancel." Using an oven mitt, "quick release"/open the steam release valve. When the steam venting stops and the silver dial drops, carefully open the lid.

3. In batches, ladle the soup into a blender taking care to only fill about half of the blender (hot liquids will expand in the blender, so please use caution). Blend on a low setting just until puréed and combined. Add the puréed soup back to the Instant Pot and press "Sauté" (reheating helps get the bubbles out of the soup), bring to a boil and give it a few stirs. Add the crème fraîche and stir until fully combined. Turn off the Instant Pot by pressing "Keep Warm/Cancel."

4. Serve immediately, topped with extra crème fraîche and a drizzle of extra-virgin olive oil.

NOTES

This soup is even better the next day—if you can wait that long.

This is an easy soup to prepare for a small dinner party. Make it a day ahead and check it off your to-make list!

Dill Soup with Yogurt

This delectable soup is full of the sweet, citrusy, aromatic flavor of dill paired with tangy cultured yogurt, creamy red potatoes and celery root.

PREP TIME: 20 MINUTES | COOK TIME: 15 MINUTES | TOTAL TIME: 35 MINUTES | YIELD: 6–8 SERVINGS

3 tbsp (43 g) grass-fed butter, ghee or avocado oil

1 leek, sliced, white and light green parts only

4 fresh garlic cloves, minced

3 fresh thyme sprigs, leaves removed and stems discarded

1½ tsp (4 g) sea salt, divided

1 lb (454 g) red potatoes, peeled and diced

1 medium celery root, outer skin removed and cut into 1" (3-cm) chunks

½ cup (26 g) chopped fresh dill

Juice of 1 lemon

4 cups (946 ml) chicken bone broth or vegetable stock

½ cup (123 g) plain whole milk yogurt

Extra-virgin olive oil, for garnish

1. Add healthy fat of choice to the Instant Pot and press "Sauté." Once the fat has melted, add the leek, garlic, thyme leaves and ½ teaspoon of the sea salt, sautéing for 5 minutes, stirring occasionally. Press the "Keep Warm/Cancel" button. Add the potatoes, celery root, dill, lemon juice, bone broth and the remaining 1 teaspoon of sea salt. Place the lid on the Instant Pot, making sure the steam release valve is sealed. Press "Soup" and decrease the time using the "-" button until you reach 10 minutes.

2. When the Instant Pot is done and beeps, press "Keep Warm/Cancel." Using an oven mitt, "quick release"/open the steam release valve. When the steam venting stops and the silver dial drops, carefully open the lid.

3. In batches, ladle the soup into a blender, taking care to fill only about half of the blender (hot liquids will expand in the blender, so please use caution). Blend on a low setting just until puréed and combined. Add the puréed soup back to the Instant Pot and press "Sauté" (reheating helps get the bubbles out of the soup), bring to a boil and give it a few stirs. Add the yogurt and stir until fully combined. Turn off the Instant Pot by pressing "Keep Warm/Cancel."

4. Serve immediately with a drizzle of extra-virgin olive oil.

> **NOTE**
> Diced cucumber adds a crunchy bite on this soup as a garnish. A dollop of sour cream or yogurt is also lovely, along with a little chopped fresh dill.

Spiced Pumpkin Soup with Cultured Sour Cream

This soup is spiced with lots of fresh ginger and orange. Gentle notes of cumin, cinnamon, cloves and turmeric accentuate the pumpkin, the true beauty of fall.

PREP TIME: 30 MINUTES | COOK TIME: 15 MINUTES | TOTAL TIME: 45 MINUTES | YIELD: 4–6 SERVINGS

4 tbsp (57 g) grass-fed butter, ghee or avocado oil

1 yellow onion, diced

3 fresh garlic cloves, minced

2" (5-cm) knob fresh ginger, peeled and finely minced or grated

5 fresh thyme sprigs, leaves removed and stems discarded

2 tsp (4 g) cumin

½ tsp ground cinnamon

¼ tsp ground cloves

¼ tsp turmeric

¼ tsp freshly ground black pepper

1½ tsp (4 g) sea salt, divided

Flesh of 2 small pie pumpkins, roasted or steamed

¾ cup (177 ml) freshly squeezed orange juice

Zest of 2 oranges

3 cups (710 ml) chicken bone broth or vegetable stock

4 oz (113 g) sour cream, for garnish

Cinnamon (optional, for garnish)

1. Add healthy fat of choice to the Instant Pot and press "Sauté." Once the fat has melted, add the onion, garlic, ginger, thyme leaves, cumin, cinnamon, cloves, turmeric, pepper and ½ teaspoon of the sea salt, sautéing for 5 minutes, stirring occasionally. Press the "Keep Warm/Cancel" button. Add the cooked pumpkin flesh, orange juice, orange zest, bone broth and the remaining 1 teaspoon of sea salt. Place the lid on the Instant Pot, making sure the steam release valve is sealed. Press "Soup" and decrease the time using the "-" button until you get to 10 minutes.

2. When the Instant Pot is done and beeps, press "Keep Warm/Cancel." Using an oven mitt, "quick release"/open the steam release valve. When the steam venting stops and the silver dial drops, carefully open the lid.

3. In batches, ladle the soup into a blender taking care to fill only about half of the blender (hot liquids will expand in the blender, so please use caution). Blend on a low setting just until puréed and combined. Add the puréed soup back to the Instant Pot and press "Sauté" (reheating helps get the bubbles out of the soup), bring to a boil and give it a few stirs. Add the sour cream and stir until fully combined. Turn off the Instant Pot by pressing "Keep Warm/Cancel."

4. Serve immediately, topped with a dollop of sour cream and a pinch of cinnamon if desired.

> **NOTE**
> Two small pie pumpkins yield about 2½ cups (290 g) of pumpkin flesh. If you don't have time to roast the pumpkins (which takes about 40 minutes to 1 hour), why not steam them in the Instant Pot? It's easy. Place the trivet tray in the Instant Pot, add 1 cup (237 ml) of water and place a whole pumpkin on top of the trivet. Place the lid on the Instant pot with the steam valve closed and set it on "Steam" for 10 minutes. This perfectly cooks the pumpkin and the skin peels off easily, too. Usually only one whole pumpkin fits in the Instant Pot, so you'll have to cook them one at a time, but you'll have two steamed pumpkins in 20 minutes!

Catalan Mushroom Soup

This elegant Mediterranean soup is full of earthy mushrooms and bursting with aromatic herby flavor. Grab some crusty bread to go with this soup because you're going to want to soak up all the broth.

PREP TIME: 20 MINUTES | COOK TIME: 21 MINUTES | TOTAL TIME: 41 MINUTES | YIELD: 6 SERVINGS

3 tbsp (43 g) grass-fed butter or ghee, divided

2 lbs (907 g) button or cremini mushrooms, halved

1 large yellow onion, sliced

1 leek, sliced, white and light green parts only

6 fresh garlic cloves, minced

5 fresh thyme sprigs, leaves removed and stems discarded

1¼ tsp (4 g) sea salt, divided

2 tbsp (8 g) chopped fresh Italian parsley, plus more for garnish

4 cups (946 ml) chicken bone broth or vegetable stock

Extra-virgin olive oil, for garnish

Shredded parmigiano-reggiano, for garnish

1. Add 2 tablespoons (29 g) of butter to the Instant Pot and press "Sauté." Once the fat has melted, add the mushrooms, sautéing for 6 minutes, stirring occasionally until lightly caramelized. Add the onion, leek, garlic, thyme leaves and ½ teaspoon of the sea salt, sautéing for 8 minutes, stirring occasionally until the onions are lightly caramelized. Press the "Keep Warm/Cancel" button. Add the parsley, bone broth and the remaining 1 teaspoon of sea salt. Give it a quick stir. Place the lid on the Instant Pot, making sure the steam release valve is sealed. Press the "Soup" setting and decrease the time using the "-" button until you reach 7 minutes.

2. When the Instant Pot is done and beeps, press "Keep Warm/Cancel." Using an oven mitt, "quick release"/open the steam release valve. When the steam venting stops and the silver dial drops, carefully open the lid.

3. Serve immediately with a drizzle of extra-virgin olive oil, a little fresh chopped Italian parsley and some shredded parmigiano-reggiano.

> **NOTE**
> This soup is delicious served with some parmesan-toasted crostini or buttered crusty bread.

Creamy Butternut Squash, Apple & Aged Cheddar Soup

Fresh spiced apple cider brings this autumnal soup to life. It's full of vibrant flavors with hints of cinnamon, cloves, cumin, sweet cider and tangy, sharp cheddar.

PREP TIME: 25 MINUTES | COOK TIME: 20 MINUTES | TOTAL TIME: 45 MINUTES | YIELD: 4–6 SERVINGS

4 tbsp (57 g) grass-fed butter or ghee

1 yellow onion, diced

3 fresh garlic cloves, minced

4 fresh thyme sprigs, leaves removed and stems discarded

1 tsp cumin

1½ tsp (4 g) sea salt, divided

1 small butternut squash, peeled, seeded and cubed

2 apples, peeled, cored and quartered

2 cups (473 ml) fresh apple cider

2 tbsp (30 ml) apple cider vinegar

2 cups (473 ml) chicken bone broth or vegetable stock

8 oz (227 g) aged cheddar cheese, shredded

Sour cream, for garnish

1. Add the butter to the Instant Pot and press "Sauté." Once the fat has melted, add the onion, garlic, thyme leaves, cumin and ½ teaspoon of the sea salt, sautéing for 5 minutes, stirring occasionally. Press the "Keep Warm/Cancel" button. Add the butternut squash, apples, apple cider, apple cider vinegar, bone broth and the remaining 1 teaspoon of sea salt. Place the lid on the Instant Pot, making sure the steam release valve is sealed. Press "Soup" and decrease the time using the "-" button until you reach 15 minutes.

2. When the Instant Pot is done and beeps, press "Keep Warm/Cancel." Using an oven mitt, "quick release"/open the steam release valve. When the steam venting stops and the silver dial drops, carefully open the lid.

3. In batches, ladle the soup into a blender taking care to fill only about half of the blender (hot liquids will expand in the blender, so please use caution). Blend on a low setting just until puréed and combined. Add the puréed soup back to the Instant Pot and press "Sauté" (reheating helps get the bubbles out of the soup), bring to a boil and give it a few stirs. Add the shredded cheese and stir until fully combined. Turn off the Instant Pot by pressing "Keep Warm/Cancel."

4. Serve immediately, topped with a dollop of sour cream.

> **NOTES**
> I like to use 1 tart green apple and 1 sweet apple in this soup.
>
> If you don't have access to fresh apple cider, use fresh apple juice. Add ¼ teaspoon of ground cinnamon, ⅛ teaspoon of ground cloves, a pinch of allspice and a pinch of freshly grated nutmeg to the Instant Pot when you add the cumin.

Tuscan Ribollita

Ribollita is a hearty Tuscan soup. It is made with day-old bread and is overflowing with vegetables, nourishing soaked white beans and herby aromatics.

INACTIVE PREP TIME: 24 HOURS | PREP TIME: 30 MINUTES | COOK TIME: 62 MINUTES | TOTAL TIME: 92 MINUTES | YIELD: 8 SERVINGS

SOAKED WHITE BEANS

½ cup (101 g) dried white beans

1 tbsp (15 ml) apple cider vinegar or lemon juice

Pinch baking soda

Filtered water

RIBOLLITA

1 loaf day-old, crusty baguette or sourdough bread, crusts removed, cut into 1" (3-cm) cubes

5 tbsp (72 g) grass-fed butter or ghee, divided

1 yellow onion, diced

6 fresh garlic cloves, minced, divided

3 fresh thyme sprigs, leaves removed and stems discarded

1½ tsp (4 g) sea salt, divided

¼ tsp crushed red pepper flakes

1 lb (454 g) dinosaur (lacinato) kale, de-ribbed and chopped

1 cup (70 g) thinly sliced savoy cabbage

28 oz (794 g) crushed or diced tomatoes

2 carrots, peeled and cut into 2" (5-cm) slices

4 cups (946 ml) chicken bone broth

¼ cup (10 g) chopped fresh basil

2 tbsp (8 g) chopped fresh Italian parsley

½ cup (50 g) shredded parmigiano-reggiano, plus more for garnish

3 tbsp (45 ml) quality extra-virgin olive oil, for garnish

1. To soak the beans, add the dry beans to a large stock pot along with 1 tablespoon (15 ml) of apple cider vinegar or lemon juice and a pinch of baking soda. Fill the stockpot with triple the amount of water as beans. Bring to a light simmer on the stove, then remove from heat, cover the pot and let the beans soak for a minimum of 8 hours, preferably overnight for 12 to 24 hours. With a spoon, remove any bubbles or scum that floats to the top. Drain and thoroughly rinse the beans in a colander.

2. Preheat the oven to 375°F (191°C). Spread the bread cubes on a baking sheet. Pour 3 tablespoons (43 g) of melted butter over the bread. Sprinkle with 2 minced garlic cloves. Using clean hands, toss the bread cubes until they are all coated. Bake for 20 minutes, remove from the oven and set aside.

3. Add 2 tablespoons (29 g) of butter to the Instant Pot and press "Sauté." Once the fat has melted, add the onion, 4 cloves of minced garlic, thyme leaves, ½ teaspoon of sea salt and red pepper flakes, sautéing for 7 minutes, stirring occasionally. Add the kale and cabbage and continue to sauté for 5 minutes, stirring occasionally. Press the "Keep Warm/Cancel" button. Add the drained and rinsed soaked beans, tomatoes, carrots, bone broth, basil, parsley and the remaining 1 teaspoon of sea salt. Stir to combine. Place the lid on the Instant Pot, making sure the steam release valve is sealed. Press the "Soup" setting, then decrease the time using the "-" button until you reach 25 minutes.

4. When the Instant Pot is done and beeps, press "Keep Warm/Cancel." Allow the Instant Pot to release pressure naturally for 5 minutes. Using an oven mitt, "quick release"/open the steam release valve. When the steam venting stops and the silver dial drops, carefully open the lid.

5. Press "Sauté" and add the parmigiano-reggiano, stirring to combine. Add the garlic toasted bread cubes and stir to combine. Once the soup starts to boil, allow it to continue boiling for 5 minutes. Turn off the Instant Pot by pressing "Keep Warm/Cancel."

6. Serve hot or warm drizzled with a generous amount of extra-virgin olive oil and freshly grated parmigiano-reggiano.

NOTES
The traditional practice of soaking beans helps reduce or neutralize phytic acid. This process helps with digestion and helps make the beans more nutrient-dense.

Creamy Calabaza-Corn Soup

Calabaza squash is similar in flavor to pumpkin or kabocha squash. It's delicious paired with corn. This creamy and silky soup is packed with sweet corn, buttery squash and herbaceous thyme and is gently spiced with cumin.

PREP TIME: 30 MINUTES | COOK TIME: 16 MINUTES | TOTAL TIME: 46 MINUTES | YIELD: 6 SERVINGS

2 tbsp (29 g) grass-fed butter, ghee or avocado oil

1 yellow onion, diced

3 fresh garlic cloves, minced

½ tsp dried thyme

½ tsp cumin

1 tsp sea salt

1 small calabaza or kabocha squash, peeled, seeded and cut into 1" (3-cm) cubes

1½ cups (246 g) fresh or frozen corn kernels

3 cups (710 ml) chicken bone broth or vegetable stock

½ cup (118 ml) cream

Fresh lime wedges, for garnish

Sour cream, for garnish

Chopped cilantro, for garnish

1. Add healthy fat of choice to the Instant Pot and press "Sauté." Once the fat has melted, add the onion, garlic, thyme, cumin and sea salt, sautéing for 6 minutes, stirring occasionally. Press the "Keep Warm/Cancel" button. Add the squash, corn and bone broth. Place the lid on the Instant Pot, making sure the steam release valve is sealed. Press the "Soup" setting, then decrease the time using the "-" button until you reach 10 minutes.

2. When the Instant Pot is done and beeps, press "Keep Warm/Cancel." Using an oven mitt, "quick release"/open the steam release valve. When the steam venting stops and the silver dial drops, carefully open the lid.

3. In batches, ladle the soup into a blender, taking care to fill only about half of the blender (hot liquids will expand in the blender, so please use caution). Blend on a low setting just until puréed and combined. Add the puréed soup back to the Instant Pot and press "Sauté" (reheating helps get the bubbles out of the soup), bring to a boil and give it a few stirs. Add the cream and stir until fully combined. Turn off the Instant Pot by pressing "Keep Warm/Cancel."

4. Serve immediately, topped with a squeeze of fresh lime juice, a dollop of sour cream and freshly chopped cilantro.

Albondigas Savory Meatball Soup with Cilantro & Mint

Albondigas is a traditional Mexican meatball soup. This comforting, brothy soup is full of vegetables and vibrant, refreshing, herby meatballs.

PREP TIME: 30 MINUTES | COOK TIME: 19 MINUTES | TOTAL TIME: 49 MINUTES | YIELD: 6 SERVINGS

MEATBALLS

1 lb (454 g) grass-fed ground beef

¼ cup (47 g) cooked white rice

¼ cup (23 g) chopped fresh mint

¼ cup (4 g) chopped fresh cilantro, plus more for garnish

1 tsp sea salt

1 pastured egg

½ yellow onion, finely chopped

SOUP

2 tbsp (29 g) grass-fed butter, ghee or avocado oil

½ yellow onion, diced

4 fresh garlic cloves, minced

1 tsp dried thyme

1 tsp cumin

1 tsp sea salt

2 tbsp (11 g) chopped fresh mint, plus more for garnish

3 zucchini, ends removed and diced

3 carrots, peeled and cut into 2" (5-cm) pieces

3 celery stalks, sliced

9 oz (255 g) diced peeled tomatoes

4 cups (946 ml) chicken bone broth or vegetable stock

1. In a large mixing bowl, combine the ground beef, rice, mint, cilantro, sea salt, egg and onion. Very gently mix until everything is evenly distributed. Roll the mixture into 2" (5-cm) meatballs. Set them aside on a plate.

2. Add healthy fat of choice to the Instant Pot and press "Sauté." Once the fat has melted, add the onion, garlic, thyme, cumin and sea salt, sautéing for 6 minutes, stirring occasionally. Press the "Keep Warm/Cancel" button. Add the mint, zucchini, carrots, celery, tomatoes and bone broth, and stir to combine. Gently place the meatballs into the soup. Place the lid on the Instant Pot, making sure the steam release valve is sealed. Press the "Soup" setting, then decrease the time using the "-" button until you reach 13 minutes.

3. When the Instant Pot is done and beeps, press "Keep Warm/Cancel." Allow to release pressure naturally for 5 minutes. Using an oven mitt, "quick release"/open the steam release valve. When the steam venting stops and the silver dial drops, carefully open the lid.

4. Serve immediately, topped with freshly chopped cilantro and mint.

Nourishing Root Vegetable Bisque with Crispy Prosciutto

If the saying "bacon makes everything better" is true, then prosciutto makes everything perfect. Especially when it's crispy! This nourishing, creamy bisque is full of winter root vegetables and topped with lots of crispy prosciutto.

PREP TIME: 30 MINUTES | COOK TIME: 21 MINUTES | TOTAL TIME: 51 MINUTES | YIELD: 6 SERVINGS

4 tbsp (57 g) grass-fed butter, ghee or avocado oil, divided

2 oz (57 g) natural (chemical- and hormone-free) prosciutto, thinly sliced into small strips

1 leek, sliced, white and light green parts only

4 fresh garlic cloves, minced

7 fresh thyme sprigs, leaves removed and stems discarded

1½ tsp (4 g) sea salt, divided

3 medium celery roots, outer skin removed and cut into 1" (3-cm) chunks

3 small turnips, peeled and cut into 1" (3-cm) chunks

3 small parsnips, peeled and cut into 1" (3-cm) chunks

3 carrots, peeled and cut into 1" (3-cm) chunks

Juice of 1 lemon

4 cups (946 ml) chicken bone broth or vegetable stock

4 oz (113 g) sour cream, plus more for garnish

Extra-virgin olive oil, for garnish

1. Add 1 tablespoon (14 g) of healthy fat of choice to the Instant Pot and press "Sauté." Once the fat has melted, add the prosciutto, sautéing for 6 minutes, stirring occasionally until crispy. Remove from the Instant Pot and transfer to a plate, set aside. Add the remaining healthy fat of choice to the Instant Pot and add the leek, garlic, thyme leaves and ½ teaspoon of the sea salt, sautéing for 5 minutes, stirring occasionally. Press the "Keep Warm/Cancel" button. Add the celery root, turnip, parsnip, carrot, lemon juice, bone broth and the remaining 1 teaspoon of sea salt. Place the lid on the Instant Pot, making sure the steam release valve is sealed. Press the "Soup" setting, then decrease the time using the "-" button until you reach 10 minutes.

2. When the Instant Pot is done and beeps, press "Keep Warm/Cancel." Using an oven mitt, "quick release"/open the steam release valve. When the steam venting stops and the silver dial drops, carefully open the lid.

3. In batches, ladle the soup into a blender, taking care to fill only about half of the blender (hot liquids will expand in the blender, so please use caution). Blend on a low setting just until puréed and combined. Add the puréed soup back to the Instant Pot and press "Sauté" (reheating helps get the bubbles out of the soup), bring to a boil and give it a few stirs. Add the sour cream and stir until fully combined. Turn off the Instant Pot by pressing "Keep Warm/Cancel."

4. Serve immediately and top with a dollop of sour cream, the crispy prosciutto and a drizzle of extra-virgin olive oil.

NOTE
For a more robust flavor, roast the root vegetable chunks prior to making the soup.

Spicy Miso Ramen

My husband is a huge ramen fan. He loves authentic ramen, not the store-bought stuff. Ramen is a work of art when you can feel the love with which it was made, starting with the homemade, flavorful broth.

PREP TIME: 25 MINUTES | COOK TIME: 1 MINUTE | TOTAL TIME: 26 MINUTES | YIELD: 2 SERVINGS

RAMEN

2 packs ramen noodles (gluten-free optional)

2 tbsp (30 ml) coconut aminos or gluten-free tamari

2 cups (473 ml) chicken bone broth

2 oz (57 g) spinach

1 tsp shiro miso paste (white fermented miso paste)

TOPPINGS

Shredded or sliced cooked meat of choice

Mushrooms, thinly sliced

Green onions, sliced on a bias

Bamboo shoots

Toasted sesame oil

Soft-boiled egg

Bean sprouts

Nori (roasted seaweed)

Chili oil and/or red pepper chili flakes

Fresh corn kernels

Toasted sesame seeds

1. Add the ramen noodles, aminos or tamari, bone broth and spinach to the Instant Pot and press the "Manual" setting, then decrease the time using the "-" button until you reach 1 minute.

2. When the Instant Pot is done and beeps, press "Keep Warm/Cancel." Using an oven mitt, "quick release"/open the steam release valve. When the steam venting stops and the silver dial drops, carefully open the lid.

3. Add the miso paste and whisk to combine.

4. Serve immediately, beautifully arranged with toppings of your choice.

NOTES

It's relatively easy to find gluten-free ramen noodles at natural food stores. Alternatively, you can purchase them online.

Roasted pork is the traditional meat used in ramen, but chicken, shrimp, etc. work well too.

Wasabi Pea Soup

Pea soup is a much-loved classic. This version takes it up a notch with the spicy kick of wasabi and the sweet flair of fresh mint.

PREP TIME: 25 MINUTES | COOK TIME: 20 MINUTES | TOTAL TIME: 45 MINUTES | YIELD: 4 SERVINGS

3 tbsp (43 g) grass-fed butter or ghee

1 yellow onion, diced

4 fresh garlic cloves, minced

2 fresh thyme sprigs, leaves removed and stems discarded

1 tsp sea salt

4 cups (252 g) fresh or frozen petite peas

1 celery stalk, sliced

1 carrot, peeled and diced

1 leaf romaine or butter lettuce, chopped

¼ cup (23 g) fresh mint, chopped

3 cups (710 ml) chicken bone broth or vegetable stock

2 tsp (7 g) prepared wasabi

½ cup (118 ml) cream

½ cup (115 g) cultured sour cream, plus more for garnish

1. Add butter to the Instant Pot and press "Sauté." Once the fat has melted, add the onion, garlic, thyme leaves and sea salt, sautéing for 7 minutes until lightly caramelized, stirring occasionally. Press the "Keep Warm/Cancel" button. Add the peas, celery, carrot, lettuce, mint, bone broth and wasabi. Place the lid on the Instant Pot, making sure the steam release valve is sealed. Press the "Soup" setting, then decrease the time using the "-" button until you reach 13 minutes.

2. When the Instant Pot is done and beeps, press "Keep Warm/Cancel." Allow the Instant Pot to release pressure naturally for 15 minutes. Using an oven mitt, "quick release"/open the steam release valve. When the steam venting stops and the silver dial drops, carefully open the lid.

3. In batches, ladle the soup into a blender, taking care to fill only about half of the blender (hot liquids will expand in the blender, so please use caution). Blend on the low setting just until puréed and combined. Add the puréed soup back to the Instant Pot and press "Sauté" (reheating helps get the bubbles out of the soup), bring to a boil and give it a few stirs. Add the cream and sour cream, stirring until fully combined. Turn off the Instant Pot by pressing "Keep Warm/Cancel."

4. Serve immediately, topped with a dollop of sour cream.

> **NOTE**
> I know the lettuce addition might seem odd. Lettuce was my mom's secret pea soup ingredient, so I have carried on that tradition.

Rustic Cabbage Soup with Soaked White Beans

Once a peasant food, this rustic, nourishing soup is simply seasoned and bursting with flavor. It uses soaked beans for better nutrition and digestion.

INACTIVE PREP TIME: 24 HOURS | PREP TIME: 20 MINUTES | COOK TIME: 32 MINUTES
TOTAL TIME: 52 MINUTES | YIELD: 6–8 SERVINGS

SOAKED WHITE BEANS

1 cup (202 g) dried white beans

1 tbsp (15 ml) apple cider vinegar or lemon juice

Pinch baking soda

Filtered water

SOUP

3 tbsp (43 g) grass-fed butter or ghee

1 leek, sliced, white and light green parts only

6 fresh garlic cloves, minced

5 fresh thyme sprigs, leaves removed and stems discarded

1½ tsp (4 g) sea salt

1 lb (454 g) savoy cabbage, thickly sliced

2 carrots, peeled and cut into large 2" (5-cm) pieces

1-oz (28-g) chunk of parmigiano-reggiano

4 cups (946 ml) chicken bone broth or vegetable stock

1. To soak the beans, add the dry beans to a large stock pot along with 1 tablespoon (15 ml) of apple cider vinegar or lemon juice and a pinch of baking soda. Fill the stockpot with triple the amount of water as beans. Bring to a light simmer on the stove, then remove from heat, cover the pot and let the beans soak for a minimum of 8 hours, preferably overnight for 12 to 24 hours. With a spoon, remove any bubbles or scum that floats to the top. Drain and rinse the beans in a colander, making sure to rinse them thoroughly.

2. Add the butter to the Instant Pot and press "Sauté." Once the fat has melted, add the leek, garlic, thyme and sea salt, sautéing for 7 minutes, stirring occasionally until lightly caramelized. Press the "Keep Warm/Cancel" button. Add the drained and rinsed soaked beans, cabbage, carrots, parmesan chunk and the bone broth in that order. Place the lid on the Instant Pot, making sure the steam release valve is sealed. Press the "Soup" setting, then decrease the time using the "-" button until you reach 25 minutes.

3. When the Instant Pot is done and beeps, press "Keep Warm/Cancel." Allow the Instant Pot to release pressure naturally for 5 minutes. Using an oven mitt, "quick release"/open the steam release valve. When the steam venting stops and the silver dial drops, carefully open the lid.

4. Serve immediately.

> **NOTE**
> For a special touch, garnish the soup with crispy pastured bacon.

Provençal Vegetable Soup with Pistou

This classic French country vegetable soup brims with hearty vegetables and is topped with a vibrant, refreshing pistou (homemade pesto). Traditionally, this soup would simmer on the stove for hours, but it takes only 13 minutes in the Instant Pot.

PREP TIME: 35 MINUTES | COOK TIME: 13 MINUTES | TOTAL TIME: 48 MINUTES | YIELD: 6–8 SERVINGS

SOUP

3 tbsp (43 g) grass-fed butter or ghee

1 yellow onion, diced

1 leek, white and light green parts only, sliced

6 fresh garlic cloves, minced

5 fresh thyme sprig, leaves removed and stems discarded

1½ tsp (4 g) sea salt, divided

6 oz (170 g) fresh button or cremini mushrooms, sliced

3 russet potatoes, peeled and diced

1 large turnip, peeled and diced

2 carrots, peeled and cut into 2" (5-cm) pieces

2 celery stalks, sliced

½ lb (230 g) green beans, ends trimmed

5 oz (142 g) crushed tomatoes

1 oz (28 g) parmigiano-reggiano

¼ cup (15 g) chopped Italian parsley

5 cups (1 L) chicken bone broth

1 cup (105 g) dried pasta, any small variety, such as elbows or shells

PISTOU

2 cups (40 g) fresh basil

2 fresh garlic cloves, peeled and sliced

Zest and juice of 1 lemon

3 tbsp (45 ml) good-quality extra-virgin olive oil

5 oz (142 g) parmigiano-reggiano, cut into chunks

½ tsp sea salt

1. Add the butter to the Instant Pot and press "Sauté." Once the fat has melted, add the onion, leek, garlic, thyme leaves and ½ teaspoon of sea salt, sautéing for 7 minutes until lightly caramelized, stirring occasionally. Press the "Keep Warm/Cancel" button. Add the mushrooms, potatoes, turnip, carrots, celery, green beans, crushed tomatoes, parmigiano-reggiano, parsley, bone broth, pasta and the remaining 1 teaspoon sea salt. Place the lid on the Instant Pot, making sure the steam release valve is sealed. Press the "Soup" setting and decrease the time using the "-" button until you reach 6 minutes.

2. While the soup cooks, add all the pistou ingredients to a food processor. Pulse until combined and smooth. Set aside.

3. When the Instant Pot is done and beeps, press "Keep Warm/Cancel." Allow the Instant Pot to release pressure naturally for 5 minutes. Using an oven mitt, "quick release"/open the steam release valve. When the steam venting stops and the silver dial drops, carefully open the lid.

4. Serve immediately topped with pistou, with crusty buttered bread on the side.

Borscht with Cultured Sour Cream

Borscht is a popular traditional soup in many cultures and is usually described as a sour and deliciously savory soup. It has a deep red hue from the earthy beets, and it's full of tender meat, sweet cabbage and lots of grassy dill.

PREP TIME: 25 MINUTES | COOK TIME: 50 MINUTES | TOTAL TIME: 75 MINUTES | YIELD: 4 SERVINGS

3 tbsp (43 g) grass-fed butter, ghee or avocado oil, divided

1 lb (454 g) grass-fed beef stew meat, cut into 1" (3-cm) cubes

1½ tsp (4 g) sea salt, divided

1 yellow onion, diced

4 fresh garlic cloves, minced

2 beets, peeled and cut into ½" (1.3-cm) cubes

2 russet potatoes, peeled and cut into ½" (1.3-cm) cubes

¼ of a small cabbage, thinly sliced

2 fresh bay leaves

1 tbsp (16 g) tomato paste

1 tbsp (15 ml) maple syrup or honey

1 cup (52 g) chopped fresh dill, plus more for garnish

4 cups (946 ml) beef bone broth

1 cup (121 g) cultured sour cream, for garnish

1. Add 2 tablespoons (29 g) of healthy fat of choice to the Instant Pot and press "Sauté." Once the fat has melted, add the stew meat, sprinkle with ½ teaspoon of sea salt and brown on each side, about 5 minutes (you might have to do this in two batches). Remove the browned stew meat, transfer to a plate and set aside. Add the remaining 1 tablespoon (14 g) of healthy fat of choice and the onion, garlic and remaining 1 teaspoon of sea salt, sautéing for 5 minutes, stirring occasionally. Press the "Keep Warm/Cancel" button. Add the beets, potatoes, cabbage, bay leaves, tomato paste, sweetener of choice, dill and bone broth and stir to combine. Add the browned stew meat and give it a stir. Place the lid on the Instant Pot, making sure the steam release valve is sealed. Press the "Meat/Stew" setting for 35 minutes.

2. When the Instant Pot is done and beeps, press "Keep Warm/Cancel." Using an oven mitt, "quick release"/open the steam release valve. When the steam venting stops and the silver dial drops, carefully open the lid.

3. Serve immediately with a generous dollop of sour cream and fresh chopped dill.

> **NOTE**
> Don't skimp on the sour cream or dill garnish. The sour cream pairs beautifully with this soup, and the fresh dill adds a wonderful layer of flavor.

Dill Crab Bisque

Crab bisque reminds me of Bodega Bay, which was my favorite childhood vacation spot. It's even more meaningful to me today because I got married there. This cozy, luscious crab bisque has many beautiful layered flavors, but the star is sweet, grassy dill.

PREP TIME: 25 MINUTES | COOK TIME: 19 MINUTES | TOTAL TIME: 44 MINUTES | YIELD: 4 SERVINGS

3 tbsp (43 g) grass-fed butter, ghee or avocado oil

2 small shallots, diced

5 fresh garlic cloves, minced

1½ tsp (4 g) sea salt, divided

¼ cup (13 g) fresh dill, chopped, plus more for garnish

2 tbsp (8 g) fresh chopped Italian parsley

2 tsp (2 g) chopped fresh thyme leaves

1 bay leaf, fresh or dried

2 celery stalks, sliced

2 small turnips or 2 small russet potato, peeled and cut into 1" (3-cm) pieces

1 tbsp (16 g) tomato paste

1 tsp Dijon mustard or horseradish mustard

1 lb (454 g) cooked crabmeat

¼ cup (59 ml) quality dry white wine

4 cups (946 ml) fish stock or chicken bone broth

½ cup (118 ml) cream

1. Add healthy fat of choice to the Instant Pot and press "Sauté." Once the fat has melted, add the shallots, garlic and ½ teaspoon of the sea salt, sautéing for 5 minutes, stirring occasionally. Add the dill, parsley, thyme and bay leaf, stirring for 1 minute. Press the "Keep Warm/Cancel" button. Add the celery, turnips or potatoes, tomato paste, mustard, crabmeat, white wine, fish stock and the remaining 1 teaspoon of sea salt. Place the lid on the Instant Pot, making sure the steam release valve is sealed. Press the "Soup" setting and decrease the time using the "-" button until you reach 13 minutes.

2. When the Instant Pot is done and beeps, press "Keep Warm/Cancel." Using an oven mitt, "quick release"/open the steam release valve. When the steam venting stops and the silver dial drops, carefully open the lid.

3. In batches, ladle the soup into a blender, taking care to fill only about half of the blender (hot liquids will expand in the blender, so please use caution). Reserve 1 cup (245 ml) of the soup, making sure to get some lump crabmeat. Blend on low setting just until puréed and combined. Add the puréed soup back to the Instant Pot along with the 1 cup (245 ml) of reserved soup. Press "Sauté" (reheating helps get the bubbles out of the soup), bring to a boil and give it a few stirs. Add the cream, and stir until fully combined. Turn off the Instant Pot by pressing "Keep Warm/Cancel."

4. Serve immediately, topped with fresh chopped dill.

NOTE
Try adding a dollop of sour cream and some extra lump crabmeat as a garnish.

Traditional Chicken Bone Broth

Chicken bone broth is my "go-to" for cooking. The mild flavor works well in pretty much any savory dish. Traditionally, bone broth takes 24 hours or more to make. With the Instant Pot, it takes only 2 hours!

**INACTIVE PREP TIME: 30 MINUTES | PREP TIME: 30 MINUTES | COOK TIME: 120 MINUTES
TOTAL TIME: 150 MINUTES | YIELD: 10+ SERVINGS**

2–3 lbs (907–1361 g) chicken carcass, bones, neck or cleaned feet

2 carrots, cut into thirds

2 celery stalks, cut into thirds

5 sprigs fresh thyme

1 yellow onion, peeled and quartered

1 whole head of garlic, smashed

1 tbsp (15 ml) apple cider vinegar

Filtered water

1 tsp sea salt, or more to taste

1. Place the bones/carcass, carrots, celery, thyme, onion, garlic and vinegar in the Instant Pot. Add about 10 cups (2.4 L) of filtered water, or until the Instant Pot is about ⅔ full. (Do not fill past the "Max" fill line.) To help pull the minerals out of the bones, allow the Instant Pot to sit at room temperature for 30 minutes.

2. After the soak period is over, place the lid on the Instant Pot, making sure the steam release valve is sealed. Press the "Soup" setting and increase the time using the "+" button until you reach 120 minutes.

3. When the Instant Pot is done and beeps, press "Keep Warm/Cancel." Allow to release pressure naturally for 20 minutes. Using an oven mitt, "quick release"/open the steam release valve. When the steam venting stops and the silver dial drops, carefully open the lid.

4. Strain the bone broth and discard all the bones and vegetable scraps. Add the sea salt, stirring to dissolve. Store in glass mason jars in the refrigerator for up to 3 days, or freeze for later use.

NOTES

I like to save the carcass from chickens that have been roasted or cooked in the Instant Pot. If I'm not using a carcass right away, I store it in the freezer for when I'm ready to make more bone broth.

I like to pour some of the bone broth into ice cube trays and freeze them for later use. These are super handy when I need to add a little broth to recipes.

Traditional Grass-Fed Beef Bone Broth

I love the deeply rich flavor of beef bone broth. Roasting the bones, vegetables and aromatics before making the broth adds an extra layer of flavor.

INACTIVE PREP TIME: 30 MINUTES | PREP TIME: 15 MINUTES | COOK TIME: 160 MINUTES | TOTAL TIME: 175 MINUTES | YIELD: 10+ SERVINGS

2–3 lbs (907–1361 g) grass-fed beef bones

2 carrots, cut into thirds

2 celery stalks, cut into thirds

1 leek, halved lengthwise and cut into thirds (wash out any sand)

2 yellow onions, peeled and quartered

1 whole head of garlic, smashed

7 sprigs fresh thyme

1 small sprig rosemary (optional)

1 tbsp (15 ml) apple cider vinegar

Filtered water

1 tsp sea salt, or more to taste

1. Place the bones and carrots, celery, leek and onions on one or two baking sheets so that they lie in a single layer. Roast at 400°F (204°C) for 40 minutes, stirring occasionally. Remove from oven.

2. Carefully add roasted bones, roasted vegetables, garlic, thyme, rosemary (if using) and vinegar to the Instant Pot. Add about 10 cups (2.4 L) of filtered water, or until the Instant Pot is about ⅔ full. (Do not fill past the "Max" fill line.) To help pull the minerals out of the bones, allow the Instant Pot to sit at room temperature for 30 minutes.

3. After the soak period is over, place the lid on the Instant Pot, making sure the steam release valve is sealed. Press the "Soup" setting and increase the time using the "+" button until you reach 120 minutes.

4. When the Instant Pot is done and beeps, press "Keep Warm/Cancel." Allow to release pressure naturally for 20 minutes. Using an oven mitt, "quick release"/open the steam release valve. When the steam venting stops and the silver dial drops, carefully open the lid.

5. Strain the bone broth and discard all the bones and vegetable scraps. Add the sea salt, stirring to dissolve. Store in glass mason jars in the refrigerator for up to 3 days, or freeze for later use.

> **NOTE**
> Knucklebones are wonderful for beef bone broth. Marrowbones are fine too, but try and get at least one knucklebone in there.

Traditional Fish Stock

You can find quality fish stocks at natural food stores these days, but there's nothing like a true, mineral-rich, nutrient-dense homemade fish stock.

INACTIVE PREP TIME: 30 MINUTES | PREP TIME: 30 MINUTES | COOK TIME: 120 MINUTES | TOTAL TIME: 150 MINUTES | YIELD: 10+ SERVINGS

2–3 lbs (907–1361 g) non-oily white fish bones, spines, ribs, heads, tails

2 carrots, cut into thirds

2 celery stalks, cut into thirds

1 leek, halved lengthwise and cut into thirds (wash out any sand)

1 yellow onion, peeled and quartered

1 whole head of garlic, smashed

1 lemongrass stalk, halved lengthwise and cut into thirds

7 sprigs fresh thyme

1 bay leaf, fresh or dried

5 sprigs Italian parsley with stems, broken in half

1 tbsp (15 ml) apple cider vinegar

Filtered water

1 tsp sea salt, or more to taste

1. If possible, wash away visible blood if you're using meaty parts of the fish. It won't change the flavor drastically if you can't.

2. Place the bones/carcass, carrots, celery, leek, onion, garlic, lemongrass, thyme, bay leaf, parsley and vinegar in the Instant Pot. Add about 10 cups (2.4 L) of filtered water, or until the Instant Pot is about ⅔ full. (Do not fill past the "Max" fill line.) To help pull the minerals out of the bones, allow the Instant Pot to sit at room temperature for 30 minutes.

3. After the soak period is over, place the lid on the Instant Pot, making sure the steam release valve is sealed. Press the "Soup" setting and increase the time using the "+" button until you reach 120 minutes.

4. When the Instant Pot is done and beeps, press "Keep Warm/Cancel." Allow to release pressure naturally for 20 minutes. Using an oven mitt, "quick release"/open the steam release valve. When the steam venting stops and the silver dial drops, carefully open the lid.

5. Strain the stock and discard all the bones and vegetable scraps. Add the sea salt, stirring to dissolve. Store in glass mason jars in the refrigerator for up to 3 days or freeze for later use.

NOTE
This delicious stock works wonderfully in any seafood-based dish.

Nourishing Vegetable Stock

This vegetable stock is wonderful to have on hand for vegetarian dishes. It is made with immune-supporting shiitake mushrooms, herbs and a whole head of garlic.

PREP TIME: 35 MINUTES | COOK TIME: 15 MINUTES | TOTAL TIME: 50 MINUTES | YIELD: 10+ SERVINGS

5–7 shiitake mushrooms

3 carrots, cut into thirds

3 celery stalks, cut into thirds

1 leek, halved lengthwise and cut into thirds (wash out any sand)

1 yellow onion, peeled and quartered

1 whole head of garlic, smashed

7 sprigs fresh thyme

1 bay leaf, fresh or dried

5 sprigs Italian parsley with stems, broken in half

1 sprig marjoram (optional)

¼ tsp black peppercorns

1 strip of kombu (optional)

Filtered water

1 tsp sea salt, or more to taste

1. Place the mushrooms, carrots, celery, leek, onion, garlic, thyme, bay leaf, parsley, marjoram (if using), peppercorns and kombu (if using) in the Instant Pot. Add about 10 cups (2.4 L) of filtered water, or until the Instant Pot is about ⅔ full. (Do not fill past the "Max" fill line.) Place the lid on the Instant Pot, making sure the steam release valve is sealed. Press the "Soup" setting and decrease the time using the "-" button until you reach 15 minutes.

2. When the Instant Pot is done and beeps, press "Keep Warm/Cancel." Allow to release pressure naturally for 15 minutes. Using an oven mitt, "quick release"/open the steam release valve. When the steam venting stops and the silver dial drops, carefully open the lid.

3. Strain the stock and discard all the vegetable and herb scraps. Add the sea salt, stirring to dissolve. Store in glass mason jars in the refrigerator for up to 3 days or freeze for later use.

NOTE

Kombu is a sea vegetable that adds trace minerals. It can be found at most natural food stores.

Tantalizing Stews

No matter what the forecast is, curling up on the sofa with a bowl of hearty stew is the perfect nightcap. Making stews should be as easy and relaxing as eating them, but that doesn't mean they can't taste gourmet! The days of waiting hours for the perfectly cooked stew are over, thanks to the Instant Pot. Just combine a handful of ingredients and press a button. The hardest part is waiting a few minutes knowing that a delicious bowl of stew is on its way.

Stews are the perfect balance between soup and a full meal, leaving you happy and ready for another bowl. Chopped fresh cilantro and a big dollop of sour cream on top? Yes, please! The Beef Picadillo Chili with Sweet Raisins (page 129) in this chapter will do the job—and then some. Craving a little spicy heat? Nourishing Kimchi Bone Broth Stew (page 126) will do the trick! Want all the beautiful flavors of the sea? I've got you covered with my favorite Bouillabaisse Provençal Fish Stew (page 138).

Kimchi Bone Broth Stew

Kimchi isn't just a condiment; it's a nourishing food full of probiotic, fermented goodness. Kimchi is the star ingredient in this fiery-hot, fit-for-a-king, vegetable-dense stew.

PREP TIME: 15 MINUTES | COOK TIME: 12 MINUTES | TOTAL TIME: 27 MINUTES | YIELD: 4 SERVINGS

2 tbsp (29 g) grass-fed butter or ghee

4 fresh garlic cloves, minced

2" (5-cm) knob fresh ginger, peeled and finely minced or grated

1 tsp sea salt

16 oz (454 g) fermented kimchi, chopped only if the pieces are too large

7 button or cremini mushrooms, halved

2 medium heads bok choy, chopped

¼ cup (59 ml) coconut aminos or gluten-free tamari

¼ tsp red pepper flakes

2 cups (474 ml) chicken bone broth

1. Add the butter to the Instant Pot and press "Sauté." Once the fat has melted, add the garlic, ginger and sea salt, sautéing for 5 minutes, stirring occasionally. Press the "Keep Warm/Cancel" button. Add the kimchi, mushrooms, bok choy, coconut aminos, red pepper flakes and the bone broth. Give it a quick stir. Place the lid on the Instant Pot, making sure the steam release valve is sealed. Press the "Soup" setting and decrease the time using the "-" button until you reach 7 minutes.

2. When the Instant Pot is done and beeps, press "Keep Warm/Cancel." Using an oven mitt, "quick release"/open the steam release valve. When the steam venting stops and the silver dial drops, carefully open the lid.

3. Serve immediately.

NOTE
Kimchi is easy to find at almost all natural food stores and mainstream grocery stores. Look for a true fermented kimchi. You'll know it's the real deal if the label says "probiotics" or "fermented." For less heat, try white kimchi. It usually contains more veggies such as carrots, daikon radish and seaweed and it packs a milder heat. Spicier kimchi will look red and will contain more red chili pepper flakes.

Beef Picadillo Chili with Sweet Raisins

This flavorful Latin American stew is seasoned with spices and fragrant herbs. You'll taste sweet undertones from the raisins and salty goodness from pimento-stuffed olives and capers.

PREP TIME: 25 MINUTES | COOK TIME: 47 MINUTES | TOTAL TIME: 72 MINUTES | YIELD: 6 SERVINGS

3 tbsp (43 g) grass-fed butter, ghee or avocado oil, divided

2 lbs (907 g) grass-fed stew meat, cut into 2" (5-cm) cubes

1½ tsp (4 g) sea salt, divided

1 red onion, diced

7 fresh garlic cloves, minced

1 jalapeño, seeded and diced

2 tbsp (15 g) chili powder blend

2 tsp (4 g) ground cumin

1 tsp dried oregano

1 tsp dried thyme

¼ tsp ground cinnamon

2 tbsp (30 ml) maple syrup or honey

18 oz (510 g) crushed or diced tomatoes

½ cup (73 g) raisins

5 oz (142 g) pimento-stuffed green olives

1 tbsp (9 g) capers

1 cup (237 ml) chicken bone broth

1. Add 2 tablespoons (29 g) of healthy fat of choice to the Instant Pot and press "Sauté." Add the stew meat, sprinkle with ½ teaspoon of sea salt and brown the meat, stirring occasionally, about 5 minutes (you might have to do this in two batches). Remove the browned stew meat to a plate and set aside. Add the remaining 1 tablespoon (14 g) of healthy fat of choice, onion and garlic and the remaining 1 teaspoon of sea salt, sautéing for 5 minutes, stirring occasionally. Add the jalapeño, chili powder, cumin, oregano, thyme and cinnamon and continue to sauté for 2 minutes, giving it a good stir. Press the "Keep Warm/Cancel" button. Add the sweetener of choice, tomatoes, raisins, olives, capers and bone broth and stir to combine. Add the browned stew meat and stir. Place the lid on the Instant Pot, making sure the steam release valve is sealed. Press the "Meat/Stew" setting for 35 minutes.

2. When the Instant Pot is done and beeps, press "Keep Warm/Cancel." Using an oven mitt, "quick release"/open the steam release valve. When the steam venting stops and the silver dial drops, carefully open the lid.

3. Serve immediately.

> **NOTE**
> This chili is delicious topped with fresh cilantro, a squeeze of fresh lime juice and a dollop of sour cream or shredded cheese (or both!).

Tuscan Beef Stew

This Tuscan stew is deeply flavored with spicy garlic, dry red wine, sweet aromatics and herbal undertones. Traditional beef stews need several hours of simmering on the stove for the meat to become tender, but in the Instant Pot it takes only 42 minutes.

PREP TIME: 25 MINUTES | COOK TIME: 42 MINUTES | TOTAL TIME: 67 MINUTES | YIELD: 6 SERVINGS

3 tbsp (43 g) grass-fed butter, ghee or avocado oil, divided

2 lbs (907 g) grass-fed beef stew meat, cut into 1" (3-cm) cubes

1½ tsp (4 g) sea salt, divided

½ tsp black pepper, freshly ground

7 fresh garlic cloves, minced

1 rosemary sprig, leaves removed and chopped, stems discarded

3 fresh thyme sprigs, leaves removed and stems discarded

1 cup (237 ml) good-quality red wine

3 carrots, peeled and cut into 2" (5-cm) pieces

2 celery stalks, sliced

15 pearl onions, peeled

5 whole peeled tomatoes

1½ cups (355 ml) beef bone broth

1 tsp anchovy paste

1. Add 2 tablespoons (29 g) of healthy fat of choice to the Instant Pot and press "Sauté." Once the fat has melted, add the stew meat, sprinkle with ½ teaspoon of sea salt and pepper and brown the meat, stirring occasionally, about 5 minutes (you might have to do this in two batches). Remove the browned stew meat, transfer to a plate and set aside. Add the remaining 1 tablespoon (14 g) of healthy fat of choice, garlic, rosemary, thyme and the remaining 1 teaspoon of sea salt, sautéing for 2 minutes, stirring occasionally. Add the red wine to deglaze the pan, scraping up any browned bits with a wooden spoon. Press the "Keep Warm/Cancel" button. Add the carrots, celery, pearl onions, tomatoes, bone broth and anchovy paste and stir to combine. Add the browned stew meat and give it a stir. Place the lid on the Instant Pot, making sure the steam release valve is sealed. Press the "Meat/Stew" setting for 35 minutes.

2. When the Instant Pot is done and beeps, press "Keep Warm/Cancel." Using an oven mitt, "quick release"/open the steam release valve. When the steam venting stops and the silver dial drops, carefully open the lid.

3. Serve immediately.

North African Spicy Peanut-Chicken Stew

Buttery and warming, this mouthwatering North African–inspired stew is brimming with vegetables, winter squash, spicy ginger and creamy peanut butter.

PREP TIME: 30 MINUTES | COOK TIME: 38 MINUTES | TOTAL TIME: 68 MINUTES | YIELD: 6 SERVINGS

3 tbsp (43 g) grass-fed butter, ghee or avocado oil, divided

2 lbs (907 g) chicken wings, legs or thighs

1½ tsp (4 g) sea salt, divided

1 red onion, thickly sliced

7 fresh garlic cloves, minced

2" (5-cm) knob of fresh ginger, peeled, finely minced or grated

1 cup (258 g) all-natural, unsalted, creamy peanut butter with no added sugar or oils

1 small butternut squash, peeled, seeded and cut into 1" (3-cm) cubes

1 medium cauliflower, cut into small florets

2 cups (134 g) collard greens or dinosaur (lacinato) kale, de-ribbed and sliced into ribbons

3 tbsp (3 g) chopped fresh cilantro, plus more for garnish

4 whole peeled tomatoes, diced

2 tsp (4 g) ground cumin

½ tsp ground cinnamon

½ tsp ground coriander

⅛ tsp red pepper flakes

2 cups (473 ml) chicken bone broth

1. Add 2 tablespoons (29 g) of healthy fat of choice to the Instant Pot and press "Sauté." Once the fat has melted, add the chicken, sprinkle with ½ teaspoon of sea salt and brown the meat for about 5 minutes (you might have to do this in two batches). Remove the browned chicken, transfer to a plate and set aside. Add the remaining 1 tablespoon (14 g) healthy fat of choice, onion, garlic, ginger and the remaining 1 teaspoon of sea salt, sautéing for 5 minutes, stirring occasionally. Press the "Keep Warm/Cancel" button.

2. Add the peanut butter and stir several times to help it melt a bit. Add the squash, cauliflower, greens, cilantro, tomatoes, cumin, cinnamon, coriander, red pepper flakes and bone broth and stir to combine. Add the browned chicken and give the contents a gentle stir. Place the lid on the Instant Pot, making sure the steam release valve is sealed. Press the "Poultry" setting and increase the time using the "+" button until you reach 28 minutes.

3. When the Instant Pot is done and beeps, press "Keep Warm/Cancel." Using an oven mitt, "quick release"/open the steam release valve. When the steam venting stops and the silver dial drops, carefully open the lid.

4. Serve immediately and garnish with fresh chopped cilantro.

> **NOTE**
> Two sweet potatoes can be used in place of the butternut squash.

Marrow, Chard & Artichoke Stew

Roasted marrow makes this stew extra-nutrient-dense and super-nourishing. This brothy, gelatin-rich, beef bone broth-based stew is full of sweet greens and delicate artichoke hearts.

PREP TIME: 25 MINUTES | COOK TIME: 62 MINUTES | TOTAL TIME: 87 MINUTES | YIELD: 4–6 SERVINGS

1 center-cut grass-fed beef marrowbone

3 tbsp (43 g) grass-fed butter or ghee

1 leek, white and light green part only, sliced

4 fresh garlic cloves, minced

2 fresh thyme sprigs, leaves removed and stems discarded

1 tsp sea salt, divided

2 russet potatoes, peeled and chopped

8 oz (227 g) artichoke hearts (not marinated)

½ lb (230 g) chard, thinly sliced

¼ cup (15 g) chopped fresh Italian parsley

3 cups (710 ml) beef bone broth

2 tbsp (6 g) chopped chives, for garnish

Extra-virgin olive oil, for garnish

1. Place the marrowbone on a baking sheet. Roast at 400°F (204°C) for 40 minutes, flipping occasionally. Remove from oven and set aside.

2. Add the butter to the Instant Pot and press "Sauté." Once the fat has melted, add the leek, garlic, thyme leaves and sea salt, sautéing for 7 minutes until lightly caramelized, stirring occasionally. Press the "Keep Warm/Cancel" button. Add the potatoes, artichoke hearts, chard, parsley, roasted marrowbone and beef bone broth. Place the lid on the Instant Pot, making sure the steam release valve is sealed. Press the "Soup" setting and decrease the time using the "-" button until you reach 15 minutes.

3. When the Instant Pot is done and beeps, press "Keep Warm/Cancel." Allow the Instant Pot to release pressure naturally for 10 minutes. Using an oven mitt, "quick release"/open the steam release valve. When the steam venting stops and the silver dial drops, carefully open the lid.

4. Serve immediately topped with freshly chopped chives and a drizzle of good-quality extra-virgin olive oil.

The Art of Great Cooking With Your Instant Pot®

Wild Mushroom & Potato Stew

Woodsy wild mushrooms, creamy potatoes, caramelized leeks and fresh thyme make this delicious stew stand out. It's full of delectable flavors and elegant enough to serve to guests.

INACTIVE PREP TIME: 20 MINUTES | PREP TIME: 22 MINUTES | COOK TIME: 20 MINUTES | TOTAL TIME: 42 MINUTES | YIELD: 4–6 SERVINGS

1 cup (29 g) dried shiitake mushrooms, chopped

1 cup (29 g) dried porcini mushrooms, chopped

2 cups (473 ml) hot filtered water

3 tbsp (43 g) grass-fed butter or ghee

1 yellow onion, diced

1 leek, white and light green parts only, sliced

5 fresh garlic cloves, minced

5 fresh thyme sprig, leaves removed and stems discarded

8 oz (227 g) fresh button or cremini mushrooms, sliced

1 tsp sea salt

3 russet potatoes, peeled and chopped

1-oz (28-g) chunk of parmigiano-reggiano

3 cups (710 ml) chicken bone broth

½ cup (118 ml) cream

¼ cup (12 g) chopped chives, for garnish

1. In a large mixing bowl, add the dried mushrooms and pour the boiling water over them. Allow to soak for 20 minutes, then strain.

2. Add the butter to the Instant Pot and press "Sauté." Once the fat has melted, add the onion, leek, garlic, thyme leaves, button mushrooms and sea salt, sautéing for 7 minutes until lightly caramelized, stirring occasionally. Press the "Keep Warm/Cancel" button. Add the soaked mushrooms, potatoes, parmigiano-reggiano and bone broth. Place the lid on the Instant Pot, making sure the steam release valve is sealed. Press the "Soup" setting and decrease the time using the "-" button until you reach 15 minutes.

3. When the Instant Pot is done and beeps, press "Keep Warm/Cancel." Allow the Instant Pot to release pressure naturally for 10 minutes. Using an oven mitt, "quick release"/open the steam release valve. When the steam venting stops and the silver dial drops, carefully open the lid.

4. Add the cream, stirring until fully combined.

5. Serve immediately, topped with freshly chopped chives, with some crusty buttered bread on the side.

Bouillabaisse Provençal Fish Stew

Warm your soul with this traditional sea stew overflowing with several varieties of fish, vegetables and herbs. Grab some crusty bread, muffins or biscuits and dip them in the nourishing broth.

PREP TIME: 20 MINUTES | COOK TIME: 11 MINUTES | TOTAL TIME: 31 MINUTES | YIELD: 6 SERVINGS

5 tbsp (72 g) grass-fed butter, ghee or avocado oil

2 celery stalks, diced

1 carrot, chopped

1 yellow onion, diced

1 leek, julienned

1 celery root, peeled and roughly chopped

1 fennel bulb, including 1 green stalk and fronds, chopped

5 fresh garlic cloves, minced

1 tsp sea salt, divided

2 lbs (907 g) assorted fresh sustainable fish such as halibut, snapper, cod or sea bass, cut into 3" (7.6-cm) chunks

1 lobster tail

3 tomatoes, seeded and chopped

2 fresh bay leaves

7 fresh thyme sprigs

3 tbsp (26 g) capers

4 cups (946 ml) fish stock

Juice of 1 lemon

¼ cup (4 g) cilantro or Italian parsley, roughly chopped

Extra-virgin olive oil to drizzle

1. Press "Sauté" and add healthy fat of choice to the Instant Pot. When hot, add the celery, carrot, onion, leek, celery root, fennel, garlic and ½ teaspoon of sea salt. Cook for 5 minutes until the onions are translucent, stirring occasionally. Turn the Instant Pot off by pressing "Keep Warm/Cancel."

2. Add the assorted fish and lobster tail, tomatoes, bay leaves, thyme, capers, fish stock and remaining ½ teaspoon of sea salt to the Instant Pot. Place the lid on Instant Pot, making sure the steam release valve is sealed. Press "Soup" and decrease the cooking time using the "-" button until you reach 6 minutes.

3. When the Instant Pot is done and beeps, press "Keep Warm/Cancel." Unplug it and use an oven mitt to "quick release"/open the steam release valve. When the steam venting stops and the silver dial drops, carefully open the lid. Add the lemon juice to the stew and stir to combine.

4. Ladle the bouillabaisse into serving bowls, sprinkle with the chopped cilantro, drizzle with extra-virgin olive oil and serve immediately with your favorite crusty bread, savory muffins or biscuits.

NOTE
For a different texture, add ½ pound (227 g) of peeled and deveined fresh shrimp or about ½ cup (122 g) of sustainable canned crab. Add this when you add the fish.

Appetizing Breakfasts

Breakfast is meant to be savored. There's nothing like a weekend breakfast when you can soak up the slower pace of the day, sit by a warm fire or on a sunny patio and eat some well-prepared food. It always feels like a breath of fresh air.

Do you like breakfast for dinner? How about breakfast for breakfast, lunch AND dinner? Breakfast is hands-down my favorite meal of the day. I love that a good breakfast makes the start of the day special while nourishing the body. A warm breakfast gives mind and body a fair chance at a great day.

Soaked Maple Porridge with Caramelized Pears (page 153) is coziness in a bowl. It's the perfect meal for those who want something that's filling and not too sweet. The oats are soaked for better nutrition and digestion, which also speeds up the cooking process.

My family loves eggs en cocotte for a protein boost with every appetizing bite. These savory eggs are easy to throw together, and they cook up in just a few minutes. I've included two versions, Mushrooms & Gruyère Eggs en Cocotte (page 142) and Crab Spinach & Swiss Eggs en Cocotte (page 150). Think frittatas are only meant to be savory? Think again! Strawberry-Thyme Sweet Frittata (page 157) is the perfect dish for those with a morning sweet-tooth who want a protein punch.

Mushroom & Gruyère Eggs en Cocotte

Classic French eggs en cocotte are an easy traditional breakfast. These steamed eggs with caramelized mushrooms and slightly salty, creamy gruyère are perfectly cooked in minutes.

PREP TIME: 10 MINUTES | COOK TIME: 8 MINUTES | TOTAL TIME: 18 MINUTES | YIELD: 3 SERVINGS

1 tbsp (14 g) grass-fed butter or ghee

3 mushrooms, sliced

¼ tsp dried thyme

3 tbsp (44 ml) cream

3 pastured eggs

2 oz (57 g) gruyère cheese, shredded

½ tsp sea salt

1 cup (237 ml) water

Freshly cracked black pepper, for garnish

1. Add the butter to the Instant Pot and press "Sauté." Once the fat has melted, add the mushrooms and thyme, sautéing for 6 minutes, stirring occasionally until lightly caramelized. Press the "Keep Warm/Cancel" button.

2. Grease 3 ramekin dishes with butter. Evenly distribute the mushroom-thyme mixture in the ramekins. Add 1 tablespoon (15 ml) of cream to each ramekin. Crack 1 egg into each ramekin. Evenly distribute the shredded cheese and sea salt on top of the eggs. Place the trivet inside the Instant Pot. Pour 1 cup (237 ml) of water into the Instant Pot. Carefully transfer the egg-filled ramekins to the Instant Pot on top of the trivet. Place the lid on the Instant Pot, making sure the steam release valve is sealed. Press "Manual," LOW pressure setting and decrease the time using the "-" button until you reach 2 minutes.

3. When the Instant Pot is done and beeps, press "Keep Warm/Cancel." Using an oven mitt, "quick release"/open the steam release valve. When the steam venting stops and the silver dial drops, carefully open the lid.

4. Serve immediately, garnished with freshly cracked black pepper.

> **NOTE**
> The eggs will end up perfectly "soft-boiled" with a runny yolk. When you use pastured eggs, you benefit from the nutrient-dense yolks.

Herbes de Provence Gruyère Kale & Mushroom Strata

A strata is a layered casserole dish made with bread, eggs and cheese. This comforting breakfast strata is brimming with caramelized mushrooms, sautéed kale and creamy gruyère and is deeply flavored with aromatic herbs de Provence.

PREP TIME: 25 MINUTES | COOK TIME: 47 MINUTES | TOTAL TIME: 72 MINUTES | YIELD: 6 SERVINGS

3 tbsp (43 g) grass-fed butter or ghee, plus some butter for greasing dish

4 fresh garlic cloves, grated or finely minced

8 oz (227 g) button or cremini mushrooms, sliced

½ lb (230 g) dinosaur (lacinato) kale, de-ribbed and cut into ribbons

2 tsp (2 g) fresh thyme, finely chopped

1 tsp herbes de Provence

1½ tsp (4 g) sea salt, divided

3 pastured eggs

1 cup (237 ml) whole milk

1 loaf of day-old bread, cut into 1" (3-cm) cubes

1½ cups (162 g) shredded gruyère

1½ cups (355 ml) water

1. Add the butter to the Instant Pot and press "Sauté." Once the fat has melted, add the garlic and mushrooms, sautéing for 6 minutes, stirring occasionally until lightly caramelized. Add the kale, thyme, herbes de Provence and ½ teaspoon of sea salt, stirring for 6 minutes until the kale is wilted. Press the "Keep Warm/Cancel" button.

2. With butter, grease a 1½-quart (1.5-L) casserole dish (I use one with a glass lid) that fits inside the Instant Pot. Set aside. In a very large mixing bowl, whisk eggs and milk together until fully incorporated. Add the bread cubes, shredded cheese, veggie mixture and remaining 1 teaspoon of sea salt, gently stirring to fully combine. Pour the mixture into the greased casserole dish. Place the glass lid on the casserole dish. Place the trivet inside the Instant Pot. Pour 1½ cups (355 ml) of water into the Instant Pot. Carefully transfer the covered casserole dish to the Instant Pot on top of the trivet. Place the lid on the Instant Pot, making sure the steam release valve is sealed. Press the "Manual" setting for 30 minutes.

3. When the Instant Pot is done and beeps, press "Keep Warm/Cancel." Allow the Instant Pot to release pressure naturally for 15 minutes. Using an oven mitt, "quick release"/open the steam release valve. When the steam venting stops and the silver dial drops, carefully open the lid.

4. Carefully remove the casserole dish from the Instant Pot and remove the lid. Optional but highly recommended: Place the casserole dish under a preheated broiler for about 3 to 5 minutes to crisp the top of the strata. Serve immediately.

NOTES

Gluten-free breads are easy to find at almost all natural food stores, as well as some mainstream grocery stores. A crusty baguette or sourdough are my favorites for this recipe, but a good-quality white bread will work well too.

You will need a 1½-quart (1.5-L) casserole dish or heat-safe glass or stainless steel bowl that fits the Instant Pot for this strata. You will also need a lid. I use a casserole dish that comes with a glass lid. If you don't have a lid for your dish or bowl, you can place a piece of parchment paper over the top of the strata, then secure it with foil.

Sausage & Gouda Breakfast Pudding

This breakfast pudding is loaded with sweet sausage, mild and buttery gouda and herby aromatics. With a creamy, custardy texture, it's perfect for entertaining and cozy enough to share with your loved ones by the fire.

PREP TIME: 25 MINUTES | COOK TIME: 48 MINUTES | TOTAL TIME: 73 MINUTES | YIELD: 6 SERVINGS

5 tbsp (72 g) grass-fed butter or ghee, divided, plus some butter for greasing dish

½ lb (230 g) sweet or mildly spicy pork sausage, casings removed

1 yellow onion, diced

3 fresh garlic cloves, grated or finely minced

4 oz (113 g) spinach

¼ cup (15 g) finely chopped fresh Italian parsley, plus more for garnish

2 tsp (2 g) finely chopped fresh thyme

1½ tsp (4 g) sea salt, divided

5 pastured eggs

1 cup (237 ml) cream

1¼ cup (142 g) shredded gouda

1 cup (113 g) shredded cheddar cheese

1 loaf of bread, cut into 1" (3-cm) cubes

1½ cups (355 ml) water

1. Add 2 tablespoons (29 g) of butter to the Instant Pot and press "Sauté." Once the fat has melted, add the sausage and sauté for about 5 minutes, stirring to break the meat into small clumps, until the sausage is not pink anymore. Transfer the sausage to a plate and set aside. Add 3 tablespoons (43 g) of healthy fat of choice to the Instant Pot and add the onion and garlic, sautéing for 5 minutes. Add the spinach, parsley, thyme and ½ teaspoon of sea salt, stirring for 3 minutes until the spinach is wilted. Press the "Keep Warm/Cancel" button.

2. With butter, grease a 1½-quart (1.5-L) casserole dish (I use one with a glass lid) that fits inside the Instant Pot. Set aside.

3. In a very large mixing bowl, whisk eggs and cream together until fully incorporated. Add the sausage, onion-garlic-spinach mixture, shredded cheeses, bread cubes and the remaining 1 teaspoon of sea salt, gently stirring to fully combine. Pour the mixture into a greased casserole dish, carefully packing the bread cubes down into the dish so they are fully saturated with the creamy egg mixture. Place the glass lid on top of the casserole dish. Place the trivet inside the Instant Pot. Pour 1½ cups (355 ml) of water into the Instant Pot. Carefully transfer the covered casserole dish to the Instant Pot on top of the trivet. Place the lid on the Instant Pot, making sure the steam release valve is sealed. Press the "Manual" setting and increase the time using the "+" button until you reach 30 minutes.

4. When the Instant Pot is done and beeps, press "Keep Warm/Cancel." Allow the Instant Pot to release pressure naturally for 15 minutes. Using an oven mitt, "quick release"/open the steam release valve. When the steam venting stops and the silver dial drops, carefully open the lid.

5. Carefully remove the casserole dish from the Instant Pot and remove the lid. Optional: Place the casserole dish under a preheated broiler for about 3 to 5 minutes to crisp the top of the bread pudding.

6. Serve immediately, garnished with freshly chopped Italian parsley.

> **NOTES**
> You will need a 1½-quart (1.5-L) casserole dish or heat-safe glass or stainless steel bowl that fits the Instant Pot for this bread pudding. You will also need a lid. I use a casserole dish that comes with a glass lid. If you don't have a lid for your dish or bowl, you can place a piece of parchment paper over the top of the bread pudding, then secure it with foil.

Aged Cheddar & Fresh Herb Savory Rice Pudding

Sometimes we just need a satisfying bowl of savory rice pudding. This creamy pudding is packed with fragrant, fresh herbs. It's pure comfort in a bowl.

PREP TIME: 25 MINUTES | COOK TIME: 22 MINUTES | TOTAL TIME: 47 MINUTES | YIELD: 6 SERVINGS

2 tbsp (29 g) grass-fed butter or ghee

2 fresh garlic cloves, minced

1 cup (200 g) basmati, jasmine or short-grain white rice

2 cups (473 ml) milk

2 cups (473 ml) filtered water

1 tsp sea salt

1 tbsp (3 g) finely minced fresh thyme leaves

1 tbsp (4 g) finely minced fresh Italian parsley

1 tbsp (2 g) finely minced fresh rosemary

1 tbsp (2 g) finely minced fresh sage

1 tbsp (3 g) finely minced fresh dill

4 oz (113 g) shredded aged or sharp cheddar cheese

1. Add 2 tablespoons (29 g) of butter to the Instant Pot and press "Sauté." Once the fat has melted, add the garlic, stirring occasionally for 2 minutes. Press the "Keep Warm/Cancel" button.

2. Place the rice in a fine-mesh colander or strainer, rinsing several times under water. Transfer the rinsed rice to the Instant Pot. Add the milk, water, salt and all the herbs. Give it a quick stir, just enough to incorporate. Place the lid on the Instant Pot, making sure the steam release valve is sealed. Press the "Porridge" setting for 20 minutes.

3. When the Instant Pot is done and beeps, press "Keep Warm/Cancel." Allow the Instant Pot to release pressure naturally for about 12 to 15 minutes. Using an oven mitt, open the steam release valve and allow any leftover pressure release. When the silver dial drops, carefully open the lid.

4. Add the cheese, stirring to combine.

5. Serve warm as is, with shredded cheese on top or with an extra pat of grass-fed butter on top.

NOTE
This rice pudding is perfect on its own and is also delicious served with breakfast sausages and fresh seasonal fruit.

Crab, Spinach & Swiss Eggs en Cocotte

This quintessential French eggs en cocotte combines perfectly steamed eggs, succulent crabmeat, garlicky spinach, nutty Swiss cheese and a hint of refreshing lemon. Creamy and rich, this breakfast is the perfect elegant weekend brunch.

PREP TIME: 15 MINUTES | COOK TIME: 9 MINUTES | TOTAL TIME: 24 MINUTES | YIELD: 3 SERVINGS

2 tbsp (29 g) grass-fed butter or ghee

1 garlic clove, grated or finely minced

3 oz (85 g) spinach

2 tsp (1 g) fresh Italian parsley, finely chopped, plus more for garnish

Zest of 1 lemon

6 oz (170 g) crabmeat

3 tbsp (44 ml) cream

3 pastured eggs

2 oz (57 g) Swiss cheese, shredded

½ tsp sea salt

1 cup (237 ml) water

Freshly cracked black pepper, for garnish

1. Add butter to the Instant Pot and press "Sauté." Once the fat has melted, add the garlic and spinach, sautéing for 7 minutes, stirring until the spinach is wilted. Press the "Keep Warm/Cancel" button.

2. Grease 3 ramekin dishes with butter. Evenly distribute the garlic-spinach mixture in the ramekins. Evenly distribute the parsley, lemon zest and crabmeat in the ramekins. Add 1 tablespoon (15 ml) of cream to each ramekin. Crack 1 egg into each ramekin. Evenly distribute the shredded cheese and sea salt over the eggs. Place the trivet inside the Instant Pot. Pour 1 cup (237 ml) of water into the Instant Pot. Carefully transfer the egg-filled ramekins to the Instant Pot on top of the trivet. Place the lid on the Instant Pot, making sure the steam release valve is sealed. Press "Manual," LOW pressure setting and decrease the time using the "-" button until you reach 2 minutes.

3. When the Instant Pot is done and beeps, press "Keep Warm/Cancel." Using an oven mitt, "quick release"/open the steam release valve. When the steam venting stops and the silver dial drops, carefully open the lid.

4. Serve immediately, garnished with freshly cracked black pepper and freshly chopped Italian parsley.

NOTES

The eggs will end up perfectly "soft-boiled," with a runny yolk. When you eat pastured eggs, you benefit from the nutrient-dense yolks.

Make sure to look for sustainable crabmeat. Remove any cracked shells when you're adding the crabmeat to the ramekins.

Soaked Maple Porridge with Caramelized Pears

Naturally sweetened porridge is a cozy treat. Jazz up this healthy breakfast with delectable caramelized pears and you'll keep your belly full and satisfied until lunch. Make sure to soak the oats for better digestion and nutrition.

INACTIVE PREP TIME: 24 HOURS | PREP TIME: 10 MINUTES | COOK TIME: 6 MINUTES | TOTAL TIME: 16 MINUTES | YIELD: 6 SERVINGS

PORRIDGE

2 cups (180 g) gluten-free rolled oats

4 cups (946 ml) filtered water, divided

2 tbsp (30 ml) organic unfiltered apple cider vinegar, lemon juice, kefir or whey

2 tbsp (29 g) grass-fed butter, ghee, avocado oil or coconut oil

2 small pears, peeled, cored, halved and sliced

½ cup (72 g) dried currants

¼ cup (50 g) maple sugar or maple syrup

2 tsp (10 ml) vanilla extract

1 tsp ground cinnamon

¼ tsp sea salt

⅛ tsp freshly grated nutmeg, optional

CINNAMON MAPLE GLAZE

2 tbsp (29 g) grass-fed butter or ghee, melted

¼ cup (50 g) maple sugar

1 tsp ground cinnamon

1. 24 hours before you want to make the porridge, place the oats in a 1-quart (1-L) jar or large glass bowl with a lid. Heat 2½ cups (593 ml) of water just until warm (do not simmer or boil). It should be warmer than room temperature, but not too hot to touch. Pour the warm water over the oats. Add your culture of choice: unfiltered apple cider vinegar, lemon juice, etc. Mix with a spoon and cover the oats with a lid. Leave the oats out on the counter, out of sunlight, for 24 hours.

2. Press "Sauté" and add 2 tablespoons (29 g) of healthy fat of choice to the Instant Pot. When the fat has melted, add the sliced pears. Cook just until lightly caramelized, about 3 minutes. Turn the Instant Pot off by pressing "Keep Warm/Cancel." Remove the pears from the Instant Pot and set aside. Leave the remaining melted fat in the Instant Pot.

3. Add the soaked oats mixture, 1½ cups (355 ml) of water, dried currants, maple sugar or syrup, vanilla extract, cinnamon, sea salt and nutmeg (if using) to the Instant Pot. Stir with a wooden spoon. Place the lid on the Instant Pot, making sure the steam release valve is sealed. Press "Manual" and decrease the time using the "-" button until you reach 3 minutes.

4. When the Instant Pot is done and beeps, press "Keep Warm/Cancel" and unplug it. Use an oven mitt to "quick release"/open the steam release valve. When the steam venting stops and the silver dial drops, carefully open the lid.

5. To make the cinnamon maple glaze, combine the melted butter or ghee with the maple sugar and cinnamon. Stir well.

6. Serve the porridge immediately, topped with cinnamon maple glaze and caramelized pears.

NOTES

If you can't find maple sugar, you can substitute another granulated sugar like brown sugar or muscovado unrefined cane sugar.

If you'd like to skip the oats-soaking process, I'd recommend using the Instant Pot "Porridge" setting for cooking instead. (Do not use the Manual setting as described, or the oats will not be cooked properly).

Lemon-Raspberry Breakfast Strata

What better way to start your morning with a serving of fruit than with a delicious, protein-packed breakfast strata? This dish is full of tart raspberries and a hint of refreshing lemon and is lovely topped with a dollop of Greek yogurt and a drizzle of maple syrup.

PREP TIME: 25 MINUTES | COOK TIME: 25 MINUTES | TOTAL TIME: 50 MINUTES | YIELD: 6 SERVINGS

3 tbsp (43 g) grass-fed butter or ghee, melted, plus some butter for greasing dish

4 oz (113 g) cream cheese, room temperature

4 pastured eggs, room temperature

2 cups (473 ml) whole milk

½ cup (165 g) honey or maple syrup, warmed

1 loaf of day-old bread, cut into 1" (3-cm) cubes

Juice and zest of 1 lemon

1 tsp vanilla extract

2½ cups (308 g) fresh raspberries, divided

1½ cups (355 ml) water

1. With butter, grease a 1½-quart (1.5-L) casserole dish (I use one with a glass lid) that fits inside the Instant Pot. Set aside.

2. Add the butter, cream cheese and eggs to a very large mixing bowl. Break the egg yolks with a spatula or wooden spoon and stir the mixture to fully combine. Add the milk and honey or maple syrup and stir to combine. Pour the bread cubes into the mixing bowl, then add the lemon juice, lemon zest, vanilla extract and 2 cups (246 g) of the raspberries. Using a spatula, gently fold and mix all the ingredients together.

3. Pour the mixture into a greased casserole dish. Place the glass lid on top of the casserole dish. Place the trivet inside the Instant Pot. Pour 1½ cups (355 ml) of water into the Instant Pot. Carefully transfer the covered casserole dish to the Instant Pot on top of the trivet. Place the lid on the Instant Pot, making sure the steam release valve is sealed. Press the "Manual" setting and decrease the time using the "-" button until you reach 20 minutes.

4. When the Instant Pot is done and beeps, press "Keep Warm/Cancel." Allow the Instant Pot to release pressure naturally for 15 minutes. Using an oven mitt, "quick release"/open the steam release valve. When the steam venting stops and the silver dial drops, carefully open the lid.

5. Carefully remove the casserole dish from the Instant Pot and remove the lid. Optional but highly recommended: Place the casserole dish under a preheated broiler for about 3 to 5 minutes to crisp the top of the strata.

6. Serve immediately and top with the remaining ½ cup (62 g) fresh raspberries.

NOTES
Gluten-free breads are easy to find at almost all natural food stores, as well as some mainstream grocery stores. A crusty baguette or sourdough is my favorite for this recipe, but a good-quality white bread will work well, too.

You will need a 1½-quart (1.5-L) casserole dish or heat-safe glass or stainless steel bowl that fits the Instant Pot for this strata. You will also need a lid. I use a casserole dish that comes with a glass lid. If you don't have a lid for your dish or bowl, you can place a piece of parchment paper over the top of the strata, then cover and secure it with foil.

Strawberry-Thyme Sweet Frittata

Change up your usual breakfast or brunch routine with this sweet frittata. A frittata is usually a savory meal, but it's also delicious with a sweeter twist. This frittata is packed full of juicy strawberries, aromatic lemony thyme and bits of creamy sheep's milk feta.

PREP TIME: 25 MINUTES | COOK TIME: 20 MINUTES | TOTAL TIME: 45 MINUTES | YIELD: 4 SERVINGS

2 tbsp (29 g) grass-fed butter or ghee, melted, plus some butter for greasing dish

4 pastured eggs, room temperature

¼ cup (59 ml) cream

¼ cup (59 ml) maple syrup or honey, warmed

1½ cups (249 g) diced or sliced strawberries

Zest of 1 lemon

1 tsp vanilla extract

3 sprigs thyme, leaves removed and stems discarded

½ cup (75 g) crumbled sheep's milk feta cheese

1 cup (237 ml) water

1. With butter, grease a 1½-quart (1.5-L) casserole dish (I use one with a glass lid) that fits inside the Instant Pot. Set aside.

2. Add the butter, eggs, cream and maple syrup or honey to a large mixing bowl. Break the egg yolks with a whisk and stir to fully combine. Add the lemon zest, vanilla extract, thyme leaves and strawberries. Using a spatula, gently fold and mix all the ingredients together.

3. Pour the mixture into the greased casserole dish. Evenly drop little crumbles of feta into the filling. Place the glass lid on top of the casserole dish. Place the Instant Pot trivet inside the Instant Pot. Pour 1 cup (237 ml) of water into the Instant Pot. Carefully transfer the covered casserole dish to the Instant Pot on top of the trivet. Place the lid on the Instant Pot, making sure the steam release valve is sealed. Press the "Manual" setting and decrease the time using the "-" button until you reach 20 minutes.

4. When the Instant Pot is done and beeps, press "Keep Warm/Cancel." Allow the Instant Pot to release pressure naturally for 10 minutes. Using an oven mitt, "quick release"/open the steam release valve. When the steam venting stops and the silver dial drops, carefully open the lid.

5. Carefully remove the casserole dish from the Instant Pot and remove the lid.

6. Serve hot or warm.

> **NOTE**
> You will need a 1½-quart (1.5-L) casserole dish or a 6-cup (1.5-L) heat-safe glass or stainless steel bowl that fits in the Instant Pot. You will also need a lid. I use a casserole dish that comes with a glass lid. If you don't have a lid for your dish or bowl, you can place a piece of parchment paper over the top, then cover and secure it with foil.

Heavenly Sweet Treats

Life is too short for missing out on occasional treats! Everyone loves to celebrate with luscious desserts—whether because of a holiday, a party, a birthday, a romantic date or simply just because.

Food makes us happy and should be enjoyed. While breakfast is my favorite meal of the day, I love sweets above all else! In fact, I have been known to enjoy dessert with breakfast on many occasions.

Desserts have been part of my life since my southern grandma taught me to bake as a very young girl. I had no idea that such delicacies could be made perfectly in an Instant Pot until I made my first Instant Pot cheesecake. In my humble opinion the Instant Pot makes a better cheesecake than any other, baked or no-bake. In fact, I'm enjoying a piece of Rose-Scented Cheesecake with Chocolate Ganache (page 172) as I write this.

From Traditional Chocolate-Orange Custard (page 168) to Cranberry-Spiced Pears (page 167), the scrumptious desserts in this chapter will be sure to please, with bliss in every bite.

Rose-Infused Spiced Rice Pudding

Floral rosewater notes, exotic cardamom and spicy cinnamon infuse this creamy, sticky pudding. With sweet raisins and crunchy pistachios, this delicate, luscious rice dessert whispers pure love.

PREP TIME: 20 MINUTES | COOK TIME: 20 MINUTES | TOTAL TIME: 40 MINUTES | YIELD: 6 SERVINGS

1 cup (185 g) basmati rice

2¼ cups (532 ml) milk

1¼ cups (296 ml) filtered water

¼ cup (59 ml) maple syrup, honey or maple sugar

½ tsp ground cinnamon

¼ tsp ground cardamom

½ cup (355 ml) very cold cream

1 tsp rosewater

1 tsp vanilla extract

¼ tsp almond extract (optional)

2 tbsp (30 ml) fresh orange juice

Zest of 1 orange

½ cup (75 g) raisins (optional)

3 tbsp (28 g) shelled pistachios, whole or roughly chopped, for garnish

1 tsp dried organic rose petals, for garnish

1. Place the rice in a fine mesh colander or strainer, rinsing several times under water. Transfer the rinsed rice to the Instant Pot. Add the milk, water, sweetener of choice, cinnamon and cardamom. Give it a quick stir, just enough to incorporate. Place the lid on the Instant Pot, making sure the steam release valve is sealed. Press the "Porridge" setting for 20 minutes.

2. When the Instant Pot is done and beeps, press "Keep Warm/Cancel." Allow the Instant Pot to release pressure naturally for 10 to 15 minutes. Using an oven mitt, open the steam release valve and allow any leftover pressure to release. When the silver dial drops, carefully open the lid.

3. In a mixing bowl or large measuring cup, add the cream, rosewater, vanilla and almond extract (if using), stirring to combine. Add the orange juice and orange zest, stirring again. Immediately add this mixture to the rice pudding, stirring to combine. Add the optional raisins and give it a stir again.

4. Serve warm, topped with pistachios and organic rose petals.

NOTES

Make sure your cream is super-cold. Cold helps keep the dairy from curdling when the orange juice is added.

The almond extract is optional but highly recommended, as it adds a lovely layer of flavor.

Lemon-Thyme Ricotta Cheesecake

Every bite of rich cheesecake is meant to be savored. This silky, creamy cheesecake refreshes with hints of lemon and herbaceous thyme.

PREP TIME: 30 MINUTES | COOK TIME: 35 MINUTES | TOTAL TIME: 65 MINUTES | YIELD: 8–10 SERVINGS

CRUST

2 tbsp (29 g) grass-fed butter or ghee, melted, plus some butter for greasing dish

2 tbsp (24 g) maple sugar or organic cane sugar

1 cup (96 g) super-fine blanched almond flour

CHEESECAKE

¼ cup (85 g) honey

1 tbsp (2 g) fresh thyme leaves, finely minced

16 oz (454 g) cream cheese, softened

¼ cup (62 g) ricotta cheese

2 pastured eggs, room temperature

½ cup (96 g) maple sugar or organic cane sugar

1 tbsp (8 g) gluten-free flour, cassava flour or flour of choice

1 tsp vanilla extract

½ tsp lemon extract

½ tsp sea salt

Zest of 1 lemon

1 cup (237 ml) water

1. With butter, grease a 6" (15-cm) or 7" (18-cm) springform pan or a 1½-quart (1.5-L) casserole dish that fits in your Instant Pot. Set aside.

2. Add all crust ingredients to a mixing bowl. With clean hands, mix until completely combined. Dump the mixture into your springform pan and press down to form a packed "crust" at the bottom. Don't allow too much to go up the sides of the pan. Transfer the pan to the freezer for 15 minutes.

3. In a small saucepan, heat honey and thyme over medium high heat, bringing to a low simmer. Remove from the heat and set aside for 10 minutes.

4. Once the thyme-honey has sat for 10 minutes, make the cheesecake filling. To a blender, add the thyme-honey, cream cheese, ricotta, eggs, maple sugar, flour, vanilla, lemon extract, sea salt and lemon zest. Mix on low speed until smooth and fully combined. Pour the cheesecake filling into the frozen springform pan. Use a spoon or spatula to evenly distribute and smooth the top. Place the Instant Pot trivet in your Instant Pot. Pour 1 cup (237 ml) of water into the Instant Pot. Gently place your springform pan in the Instant Pot and cover with a casserole dish glass lid. Place the lid on the Instant Pot, making sure the steam release valve is sealed. Press the "Manual" setting and increase the time using the "+" button until you reach 35 minutes.

5. When the Instant Pot is done and beeps, press "Keep Warm/Cancel." Allow the Instant Pot to release pressure naturally for 15 minutes. Using an oven mitt, "quick release"/open the steam release valve. When the steam venting stops and the silver dial drops, carefully open the lid.

6. Remove the lid and carefully lift the trivet and the cheesecake out of the Instant Pot. Use oven mitts or thick towels because the Instant Pot and springform pan will be extremely hot. Allow the cheesecake to cool to room temperature with the lid still on. Once it has cooled, remove the lid, taking care not to drip any of the condensation onto the top of the cheesecake. Gently run a knife around the edges of the cheesecake to loosen it for when you're ready to remove it from the pan. Wipe off all condensation from the lid and place it back on top of the cheesecake. Transfer to the refrigerator for at least 4 hours until completely chilled, preferably overnight.

7. Serve chilled.

Pumpkin Pie with Jaggery Crust

Jaggery is a traditional sweetener made by evaporating raw sugarcane juice without separating the molasses from the crystals. It contains trace minerals and has a richer taste than sugar. It adds a lovely touch to traditional pumpkin pie.

PREP TIME: 30 MINUTES | COOK TIME: 35 MINUTES | TOTAL TIME: 65 MINUTES | YIELD: 8–10 SERVINGS

JAGGERY OR MAPLE CRUST

2 tbsp (29 g) grass-fed butter or ghee, melted, plus some butter for greasing dish

2 tbsp (28 g) jaggery or maple sugar

1 cup (96 g) super-fine blanched almond flour

PIE FILLING

1 cup (245 g) pumpkin purée

½ cup (118 ml) maple syrup

1 pastured egg

½ cup (118 ml) cream

Zest of 1 orange

1 tsp vanilla extract

1 tsp ground cinnamon

¼ tsp ground cloves

¼ tsp ground ginger

¼ tsp ground allspice

1 cup (237 ml) water

1. With butter, grease a 6" (15-cm) or 7" (18-cm) springform pan or a 1½-quart (1.5-L) casserole dish that fits in your Instant Pot. Set aside.

2. Add all crust ingredients to a mixing bowl. With clean hands, mix until completely combined. Dump the mixture into your springform pan and press down to form a packed "crust" at the bottom. Don't allow too much to go up the sides of the pan. Transfer the pan to the freezer for 15 minutes.

3. While the crust is chilling, make the pumpkin pie filling. In a large mixing bowl with a mixer or in a blender, add the pumpkin purée, maple syrup, egg, cream, orange zest, vanilla, cinnamon, cloves, ginger and allspice. Mix on a low speed until smooth and fully combined. Pour the pumpkin pie filling into the frozen springform pan. Use a spoon or spatula to evenly distribute and smooth the top. Place the Instant Pot trivet in your Instant Pot. Pour 1 cup (237 ml) of water into the Instant Pot. Gently place your springform pan in the Instant Pot and cover with a casserole dish glass lid. Place the lid on the Instant Pot, making sure the steam release valve is sealed. Press the "Manual" setting and increase the time using the "+" button until you reach 35 minutes.

4. When the Instant Pot is done and beeps, press "Keep Warm/Cancel." Allow the Instant Pot to release pressure naturally for 15 minutes. Using an oven mitt, "quick release"/open the steam release valve. When the steam venting stops and the silver dial drops, carefully open the lid.

5. Remove the lid and carefully lift the trivet and the pumpkin pie out of the Instant Pot. Use oven mitts or thick towels because the Instant Pot and springform pan will be extremely hot. Allow the pumpkin pie to cool to room temperature with the lid remaining on. Once it's cooled, remove the lid, taking care not to drip any of the condensation on the top of the pumpkin pie. Gently run a knife around the edges of the pumpkin pie. This will help loosen it when you're ready to remove it from the pan. Wipe off all condensation from the lid and place it back on top of the pumpkin pie. Transfer to the refrigerator for at least 4 hours until completely chilled, preferably overnight.

6. Serve chilled as-is or with homemade whipped cream or homemade vanilla or cinnamon ice cream.

Cranberry-Spiced Pears

These aromatic spiced pears are an extra-special treat. They're sweet and tangy, perfectly spiced with cinnamon and cloves. They cook to perfection in minutes.

PREP TIME: 20 MINUTES | COOK TIME: 3 MINUTES | TOTAL TIME: 23 MINUTES | YIELD: 5 SERVINGS

5 firm ripe pears, peeled

3 cups (710 ml) unsweetened cranberry juice

1 cup (237 ml) freshly squeezed orange juice

½ cup (118 ml) maple syrup, honey or maple sugar

2 cinnamon sticks

7 whole cloves

2 tsp (10 ml) vanilla extract

2 tbsp (29 g) grass-fed butter or ghee

1. Place the pears in the Instant Pot. Add the cranberry juice, orange juice, sweetener of choice, cinnamon sticks and whole cloves. Ladle some of the juice over the tops of the pears. Place the lid on the Instant Pot, making sure the steam release valve is sealed. Press the "Manual" setting and decrease the time using the "-" button until you reach 3 minutes.

2. When the Instant Pot is done and beeps, press "Keep Warm/Cancel." Using an oven mitt, "quick release"/open the steam release valve. When the steam venting stops and the silver dial drops, carefully open the lid. Add the butter to the cranberry liquid, allowing it to melt. Gently and carefully ladle the liquid over the pears.

3. Serve warm in a bowl with extra cranberry sauce over the top.

NOTES

If you'd like to reduce the sauce, remove all the pears and set aside. Turn the Instant Pot to "Sauté" and allow the cranberry sauce to come to a boil and reduce by half, about 10 minutes. The sauce will be more concentrated and slightly thicker.

These pears are delicious served slightly cooled with homemade vanilla or cinnamon ice cream or homemade whipped cream.

Traditional Chocolate-Orange Custard

This rich and decadent chocolate-orange custard is elegant enough to serve to guests and perfect to share with those you love.

PREP TIME: 25 MINUTES | COOK TIME: 6 MINUTES | TOTAL TIME: 31 MINUTES | YIELD: 6 SERVINGS

4 pastured egg yolks

⅓ cup (67 g) maple sugar, maple syrup, honey or organic cane sugar

1½ cups (355 ml) cream

¼ cup (59 ml) milk

6 oz (170 g) good-quality chocolate, melted

Zest of 1 orange

2 tbsp (30 ml) fresh orange juice

1 tsp vanilla extract

⅛ tsp sea salt

1½ cups (355 ml) water

1. In a large mixing bowl, whisk the egg yolks and sweetener of choice and set aside.

2. In a small saucepan, slowly bring the cream and milk to a low simmer, then remove from heat. Slowly whisk the hot cream into the egg-sugar mixture. Immediately whisk in the melted chocolate until fully combined. Add the orange zest and juice, vanilla and sea salt and whisk to combine. Pour the custard into 6 ramekin dishes. Place the trivet inside the Instant Pot. Pour 1½ cups (355 ml) of water into the Instant Pot. Carefully transfer 3 of the custard-filled ramekins to the Instant Pot on top of the trivet. Add a second trivet on top of the ramekins. transfer the remaining 3 ramekins on top of the trivet. Place the lid on the Instant Pot, making sure the steam release valve is sealed. Press "Manual" and decrease the timing using the "-" button until you reach 6 minutes.

3. When the Instant Pot is done and beeps, press "Keep Warm/Cancel." Allow the Instant Pot to release pressure naturally for 15 minutes. Using an oven mitt, "quick release"/open the steam release valve. When the steam venting stops and the silver dial drops, carefully open the lid.

4. Carefully remove the ramekins and allow to cool. Once they're at room temperature, place them in the refrigerator to chill and set up for at least 4 hours, preferably overnight.

5. Serve chilled.

NOTES

I use 2 Instant Pot trivets in this recipe. If you don't have a second trivet, just make the custard in two batches.

Use whatever kind of good-quality chocolate you prefer: milk chocolate, dark chocolate or bittersweet. If you're gluten-free, make sure to use allergy-friendly chocolate. Most fair-trade chocolates are gluten-free these days, but it's best to check the label.

For an elegant variation, top with homemade whipped cream, shaved quality chocolate and a little fresh orange zest. These beautiful chocolatey custards are also delicious topped with a little flaked sea salt.

Spiced Pumpkin Bundt Cake

Everyone loves the flavors of autumn. This sweet pumpkin bundt cake, moist and perfectly spiced, is sure to impress. Simple yet elegant, it is wonderful to serve to guests.

PREP TIME: 30 MINUTES | COOK TIME: 25 MINUTES | TOTAL TIME: 55 MINUTES | YIELD: 8–10 SERVINGS

½ cup (115 g) grass-fed butter, softened, plus more for greasing dish

1¼ cups (156 g) all-purpose gluten-free or regular flour

1½ tsp (4 g) ground cinnamon

1 tsp ground ginger

¼ tsp ground cloves

¼ tsp allspice

¾ tsp baking soda

¼ tsp sea salt

½ cup (96 g) maple sugar, muscovado sugar or organic cane sugar

2 pastured eggs, room temperature

1 cup (245 g) pumpkin purée

1 tsp vanilla extract

Zest of 1 orange

1½ cups (355 ml) water

1. With butter, grease a 6-cup (1.5-L) bundt cake pan that fits in your Instant Pot. If you don't have one, use a 1½-quart (1.5-L) casserole dish or 6-cup (1.5-L) heatproof bowl that fits in your Instant Pot. If you're using a casserole dish or heatproof bowl, add a circular piece of unbleached parchment paper that will fit on the bottom. Set aside.

2. In a medium mixing bowl, combine flour, cinnamon, ginger, cloves, allspice, baking soda and sea salt and set aside.

3. In a large mixing bowl with a mixer, cream the butter and sugar for 2 minutes, scraping down the sides with a spatula as needed. Add eggs and mix until combined, scraping down the sides as needed. Add the pumpkin purée, vanilla and orange zest, mixing until combined. Add the dry ingredients and mix until combined (do not overmix), scraping down the sides as needed. Pour the cake batter into the greased bundt pan. Use a spoon or spatula to evenly distribute. Place the Instant Pot trivet in your Instant Pot. Pour 1½ cups (355 ml) of water into the Instant Pot. Gently transfer your cake pan to the Instant Pot and cover with a glass casserole dish lid. Place the lid on the Instant Pot, making sure the steam release valve is sealed. Press the "Manual" setting and decrease the time using the "-" button until you reach 25 minutes.

4. When the Instant Pot is done and beeps, press "Keep Warm/Cancel." Allow the Instant Pot to release pressure naturally for 10 minutes. Using an oven mitt, "quick release"/open the steam release valve. When the steam venting stops and the silver dial drops, carefully open the lid.

5. Remove the lid and carefully lift the trivet and the bundt pan out of the Instant Pot. Use oven mitts or thick towels because the Instant Pot and bundt pan will be extremely hot. Allow the cake to cool uncovered at room temperature for 15 minutes, then gently remove it from the bundt pan and finish cooling on a wire rack.

6. Slice and serve.

NOTES

If you don't have a glass lid for your pan, dish or bowl, you can cover the top with unbleached parchment paper, then top that with foil and secure it around the edges.

For a special touch, serve this cake with homemade vanilla ice cream, homemade whipped cream or homemade cream cheese frosting, or dust it with organic powdered sugar.

Maple-Orange Crème Caramel

When I was a child, my mom made crème caramel for almost every dinner party she hosted. The guests and I were always wowed by it. This rich yet delicate maple- and orange-infused custard, with a layer of soft caramel on top, never fails to please.

PREP TIME: 25 MINUTES | COOK TIME: 7 MINUTES | TOTAL TIME: 32 MINUTES | YIELD: 6 SERVINGS

1 cup (192 g) organic cane sugar

2 tbsp (30 ml) freshly squeezed orange juice

4 pastured eggs

½ cup (118 ml) maple syrup

1½ cups (355 ml) whole milk

½ cup (118 ml) cream

1 tsp vanilla extract

Zest of 1 orange

1½ cups (355 ml) water

1. In a medium saucepan over high heat, add sugar and orange juice and watch carefully. As soon as the sugar dissolves, give the pan one twirl, but do not stir. As soon as almost all the sugar has turned to caramel, remove the pan from heat and twirl it once, until all the sugar becomes caramel. Line up 6 ramekins on a flat surface. Carefully pour a small amount of the extremely hot caramel into the bottom of each ramekin. Pick up each ramekin and twirl it so some of the caramel spreads onto the lower sides.

2. In a mixing bowl, whisk eggs and maple syrup until fully combined. Add the milk, cream, vanilla and orange zest and whisk just until combined. Pour the custard into the ramekins, leaving ½" (1 cm) of space at the top. Cover each ramekin with a small square of unbleached parchment paper, then cover the parchment paper with foil and secure around the ramekin's edges. Place the Instant Pot trivet inside the Instant Pot. Pour 1½ cups (355 ml) of water into the Instant Pot. Carefully transfer 3 of the custard-filled ramekins to the Instant Pot on top of the trivet. Add a second trivet on top of the ramekins. Transfer the remaining 3 ramekins to the top of this second trivet. Place the lid on the Instant Pot, making sure the steam release valve is sealed. Press "Manual" and decrease the time using the "-" until you reach 7 minutes.

3. When the Instant Pot is done and beeps, press "Keep Warm/Cancel." Let the Instant Pot release pressure naturally for 10 minutes. Using an oven mitt, "quick release"/open the steam release valve. When the steam venting stops and the silver dial drops, carefully open the lid.

4. Carefully remove the ramekins and allow them to cool. Once they're at room temperature, transfer the ramekins to the refrigerator to chill and set up for at least 4 hours, preferably overnight.

5. To serve, turn each ramekin upside down on a small plate. If the Crème Caramel doesn't slip right out, you may need to loosen it just a bit. Carefully run a knife around the sides of the ramekin and gently pull the knife towards the center just a bit to help release the suction.

NOTES

I use 2 Instant Pot trivets in this recipe. If you don't have a second trivet, just make the Crème Caramel in two batches.

For a special treat, top with a dollop of homemade whipped cream and some orange zest.

Sticky Toffee Pudding

Sticky toffee pudding is a timeless classic. It's packed with medjool dates, which make this delicate pudding "cake" extra moist. It is perfectly satisfying for dessert, an afternoon tea party or even for breakfast.

PREP TIME: 30 MINUTES | COOK TIME: 35 MINUTES | TOTAL TIME: 65 MINUTES | YIELD: 6–8 SERVINGS

5 tbsp (72 g) grass-fed butter, softened, plus more for greasing dish

1½ cups (360 g) pitted medjool dates, finely chopped

1 cup (237 ml) filtered water

½ cup (96 g) maple sugar, muscovado sugar or organic cane sugar

3 tbsp (63 g) organic blackstrap molasses

3 pastured eggs, room temperature

⅓ cup (79 ml) cream

1 tsp vanilla extract

1 cup (125 g) all-purpose gluten-free or regular flour

½ tsp baking soda

1 tsp sea salt

1 tsp ground ginger

¼ tsp ground cloves

1½ cups (355 ml) water

Homemade whipped cream, for garnish

1. With butter, grease a 1½-quart (1.5-L) casserole dish, 6-cup (1.5-L) bundt cake pan or 6-cup (1.5-L) heatproof bowl that fits in your Instant Pot. If you're using a casserole dish or heatproof bowl, add a circular piece of unbleached parchment paper that will fit inside on the bottom. Set aside.

2. In a medium saucepan, combine the chopped dates and water, bringing to a boil over medium heat. As soon as the mixture boils, remove from heat and set aside.

3. In a large mixing bowl with a mixer, cream the butter and sugar for 2 minutes. Add the molasses and mix just until incorporated, scraping down the sides with a spatula as needed. Add the eggs, cream and vanilla and mix until combined. Add the dry ingredients and mix until combined (do not overmix). Pour the cake batter into the greased cake pan. Use a spoon or spatula to evenly distribute and smooth the top. Place the Instant Pot trivet in your Instant Pot. Pour 1½ cups (355 ml) of water into the Instant Pot. Gently transfer your cake pan to on top of the trivet and cover with a casserole dish glass lid. Place the lid on the Instant Pot, making sure the steam release valve is sealed. Press the "Manual" setting and increase the time using the "+" button until you reach 35 minutes.

4. When the Instant Pot is done and beeps, press "Keep Warm/Cancel." Allow the Instant Pot to release pressure naturally for 20 minutes. Using an oven mitt, "quick release"/open the steam release valve. When the steam venting stops and the silver dial drops, carefully open the lid.

5. Remove the lid and carefully lift the trivet and the cake pan out of the Instant Pot. Use oven mitts or thick towels because the Instant Pot and cake pan will be extremely hot. Allow the pudding to cool uncovered at room temperature for 15 minutes.

6. Serve warm with homemade whipped cream.

NOTE
This recipe requires a 1½-quart (1.5-L) casserole dish with a glass lid, 6-cup (1.5-L) bundt cake pan or 6-cup (1.5-L) heatproof bowl. Whichever you use, just make sure it fits in your Instant Pot. If you don't have a glass lid, you can cover the top of the pan, dish or bowl with unbleached parchment paper, then top that with foil and secure it around the edges.

Gâteau au Chocolat

"Gâteau au chocolat" is a fancy way of saying "chocolate cake." This divine French cake, made with melted chocolate, is rich, decadent and very chocolaty. Hooray for cake in the Instant Pot! For a special touch, serve this cake with crème anglaise, fruit coulis, fresh fruit or homemade vanilla ice cream.

PREP TIME: 30 MINUTES | COOK TIME: 22 MINUTES | TOTAL TIME: 52 MINUTES | YIELD: 8 SERVINGS

CAKE

½ cup (115 g) grass-fed butter, softened, plus more for greasing dish

12 oz (340 g) good-quality chocolate, chopped

½ cup (96 g) maple sugar or organic cane sugar

2 tbsp (11 g) cocoa powder

¼ cup (31 g) all-purpose gluten-free or regular flour

⅛ tsp sea salt

4 pastured eggs, room temperature

1½ cups (355 ml) water

GANACHE

⅓ cup (79 ml) organic cream

6 oz (170 g) good-quality chocolate, chopped

¼ tsp sea salt

Flaked sea salt for sprinkling on top of the ganache

1. With butter, grease a 1½-quart (1.5-L) casserole dish that fits in your Instant Pot. Add a circular piece of unbleached parchment paper that will fit inside on the bottom. Set aside.

2. Add the chocolate, butter and sugar to a double boiler placed over simmering water. Melt them together over medium-low heat, stirring occasionally. Set aside.

3. To a large mixing bowl add cocoa, flour and sea salt. Using a mixer at low speed, slowly add the melted chocolate mixture and increase to medium speed. Mix just until incorporated. Add the eggs one at a time, mixing on medium speed, just until fully incorporated, scraping down the sides as needed.

4. Pour the cake batter into the greased and parchment paper-lined dish. Use a spoon or spatula to distribute evenly. Place the Instant Pot trivet in your Instant Pot. Pour 1½ cups (355 ml) of water into the Instant Pot. Gently transfer your cake pan into the Instant Pot and cover with a glass casserole dish lid. Place the lid on the Instant Pot, making sure the steam release valve is sealed. Press the "Manual" setting and decrease the time using the "-" button until you reach 22 minutes.

5. When the Instant Pot is done and beeps, press "Keep Warm/Cancel." Allow the Instant Pot to release pressure naturally for 10 minutes. Using an oven mitt, "quick release"/open the steam release valve. When the steam venting stops and the silver dial drops, carefully open the lid.

6. Remove the lid and carefully lift the trivet and the casserole dish out of the Instant Pot. Use oven mitts or thick towels because the Instant Pot and casserole dish will be extremely hot. Allow the cake to cool uncovered at room temperature for 20 minutes, then transfer it to the refrigerator. Let it chill and set up in the refrigerator for at least 30 minutes, preferably 1 to 2 hours.

7. When the gâteau au chocolat is chilled, make the chocolate ganache. Place the cream in a small saucepan and bring to a boil. Immediately remove from heat and add the chopped chocolate and sea salt. Stir until all the chocolate is melted and it's smooth and shiny. Pour over the top of the gâteau au chocolat. Use a spoon to smooth out the ganache and sprinkle the top with flaked sea salt.

8. Slice the cake, cleaning the knife between slices. (Keep a warm, wet towel handy.) Served chilled or at room temperature.

Spiced Gingerbread

Gingerbread is a classic. This deeply flavored, buttery, spicy cake is satisfying any time of day.

PREP TIME: 30 MINUTES | COOK TIME: 25 MINUTES | TOTAL TIME: 55 MINUTES | YIELD: 8–10 SERVINGS

½ cup (115 g) grass-fed butter, softened, plus more for greasing dish

1 cup (125 g) all-purpose gluten-free or regular flour

1½ tsp (3 g) ground ginger

1 tsp ground cinnamon

¼ tsp ground cloves

¾ tsp baking soda

¼ tsp sea salt

½ cup (96 g) maple sugar, muscovado sugar or organic cane sugar

¼ cup (84 g) organic blackstrap molasses

2 pastured eggs, room temperature

1 tsp vanilla extract

1½ cups (355 ml) water

1. With butter, grease a 1½-quart (1.5-L) casserole dish, 6-cup (1.5-L) bundt cake pan or 6-cup (1.5-L) heatproof bowl that fits in your Instant Pot. If you're using a casserole dish or heatproof bowl, add a circular piece of unbleached parchment paper that will fit inside on the bottom. Set aside.

2. In a medium mixing bowl, combine flour, ginger, cinnamon, cloves, baking soda and sea salt and set aside.

3. In a large mixing bowl with a mixer, cream the butter and sugar for 2 minutes. Add the molasses and mix just until incorporated, scraping down the sides with a spatula as needed. Add the eggs and vanilla and mix until combined. Add the dry ingredients and mix until combined (do not overmix). Pour the cake batter into the greased cake pan. Use a spoon or spatula to evenly distribute and smooth the top. Place the Instant Pot trivet in your Instant Pot. Pour 1½ cups (355 ml) of water into the Instant Pot. Gently transfer the cake pan to the Instant Pot and cover with a casserole dish glass lid. Place the lid on the Instant Pot, making sure the steam release valve is sealed. Press the "Manual" setting and decrease the time using the "-" button until you reach 25 minutes.

4. When the Instant Pot is done and beeps, press "Keep Warm/Cancel." Allow the Instant Pot to release pressure naturally for 10 minutes. Using an oven mitt, "quick release"/open the steam release valve. When the steam venting stops and the silver dial drops, carefully open the lid.

5. Remove the lid and carefully lift the trivet and the cake pan out of the Instant Pot. Use oven mitts or thick towels because the Instant Pot and cake pan will be extremely hot. Allow the cake to cool uncovered at room temperature for 15 minutes, then remove it from the pan and let it finish cooling on a wire rack.

6. Slice and serve.

NOTES

If you don't have a glass lid for your pan, dish, or bowl, you can cover the top with unbleached parchment paper, then top that with foil and secure it around the edges.

For a special touch, serve this cake with homemade vanilla ice cream, homemade whipped cream or homemade cream cheese frosting, or dust it with organic powdered sugar.

Dirty 12+ and Clean 15™

Sadly, most of our food supply these days is contaminated with pesticides and chemicals. The good news is that some conventional foods are safer to consume even if they're not organic. Each year the Environmental Working Group (EWG) puts out a list called The Dirty 12+ and Clean 15™. The fruits and vegetables that are most contaminated with pesticides and chemicals are the Dirty 12+, and the conventional fruits and vegetables that are safest to eat are the Clean 15. The Environmental Working Group updates these lists yearly, so make sure to check out the latest findings at www.ewg.org.

CURRENT DIRTY 12+

1. Strawberries
2. Apples
3. Nectarines
4. Peaches
5. Celery
6. Grapes
7. Cherries
8. Spinach
9. Tomatoes
10. Sweet Bell Peppers
11. Cherry Tomatoes
12. Cucumbers
13. Hot Peppers
14. Kale/Collard Greens

CURRENT CLEAN 15

1. Avocados
2. Sweet Corn*
3. Pineapples
4. Cabbage
5. Sweet Peas (frozen)
6. Onions
7. Asparagus
8. Mangos
9. Papayas*
10. Kiwi
11. Eggplant
12. Honeydew Melon
13. Grapefruit
14. Cantaloupe
15. Cauliflower

*The asterisks on the Clean 15 indicate that a small proportion of those items sold in the United States is produced from GM (genetically modified) seeds. If you want to avoid GM produce, buy organic instead.

The other good news is that organic products are becoming more affordable as more consumers are asking for them at their local grocery stores. Demand is increasing as more people learn about the dangers of pesticides, which means the prices are starting to come down. Have you checked out the prices at your local farmers' market? Sometimes you can find steals on produce that is not certified organic, but the farmers use organic practices. Many farmers cannot afford organic certification, but they still grow pesticide-free produce. They are usually happy to discuss their farming practices with you if you ask.

Acknowledgements

Since childhood, I dreamed of writing a cookbook. My mom always told me I would. And here I am, at the end of my first cookbook. Humbled, grateful and excited.

When my editor suggested I write a cookbook, tears of joy streamed down my face. My kids asked what was wrong, and I could barely catch my breath enough to say, "These are happy tears!" I had no idea how I would manage a book along with full-time blogging, writing, mommy-hood, being a good wife, keeping up with household stuff and so on, but there was no way I could turn down this opportunity. I jumped at the chance, because to reach your dreams, you have to go for it.

I could not have completed this book without the help of my husband. Rudy, thank you for everything that you have done to support me during this process. You have been my sous-chef, my sidekick, my support when I didn't know how to keep going and my number-one encourager. You brought me meals when I didn't ask, you cooked for our whole family when I didn't have the time to, you held my props when I needed you to, you let me bounce ideas off you, you played with the girls so I could get work done, you set up a desk area for me where there were fewer distractions and on and on. I cannot thank you enough for your help, your love, your support and your time. I love you so much! Thank you for being there for me.

Little Love and Tiny Love, my beautiful girls: Thank you for being my taste testers, my little assistants, my prop holders and my hug-givers. Thank you for being patient. I know I wasn't present enough at times, but I love you more than anything. You are the reason I do what I do.

To my mom Martha Criswell: You are my angel watching over me. I know you would have been so proud of me. Thank you for believing in and supporting me no matter what. I love you and miss you more than I can express.

To my mother-in-law Susana Halfon: Thank you for being such a huge support. Thank you for all the grocery trips and for the loving time you spent with the girls while I was working. I can't thank you enough.

To my dear friends who supported me with loving words of encouragement: Nicole Biegenzahn (my soul sister), for your constant support; Megan Stevens, for your wisdom and thoughtful offers; Anya Jang, for your support, your books, your props and your thoughtful gifts; Jessica Espinoza, for believing in me; and Jennifer Nitrio, for checking in with me—I'm so grateful to all of you.

To my cousin Tee Raskin: Thank you for believing in me, for our conversations about writing and for your words of love and encouragement. You were the first person to say I should write a cookbook. Thank you for helping support that vision.

To my husband's dear friend Dan Kwak: Thank you for your photography tips, for sharing your expertise and for your encouragement.

To my talented blogger friend Trisha Hughes: Thank you for answering my photography questions.

To my publisher and editor: Will Kiester and Sarah Monroe, thank you for giving me a chance. I cannot thank you enough for this opportunity. I am forever grateful.

For you, my dear, loyal readers: Thank you so much for supporting me. Thank you for taking time out of your day to connect with me on social media, for sharing your stories and for making a difference in your life by being mindful of the importance of real food, home-cooked meals and natural living.

About the Author

Emily Sunwell-Vidaurri is a water kefir– and chocolate-loving, holistic-minded wife and mommy of two. She is the founder and voice behind Recipes to Nourish (www.recipestonourish.com), a gluten-free blog focusing on real food and holistic health. Having her daughters changed her life. She became mindful of everything that went into her body and started eating real food, making home-cooked meals from scratch and living a more natural life. She stopped listening to conventional wisdom and started researching everything on her own.

As a wife and mommy dedicated to making nourishing food and using safe products for her family, she works to empower her readers by showing them that there is a healthier way to eat and live. Her passion is to make healthy, natural living as uncomplicated and enjoyable as possible. She and her family live in Sacramento, California.

Index